Entertainment WEEKLY

Collector's Edition

FRIENDS

THE ULTIMATE EPISODE GUIDE

CONTENTS

The cast—(from left) Matthew Perry, Lisa Kudrow, David Schwimmer, Courteney Cox, Jennifer Aniston and Matt LeBlanc—take a final bow in 2004.

FOREWORD

Friends Forever

How the beloved series became Must See TV in the '90s—and then again, long after its run on NBC concluded. *By Amy Wilkinson*

IT'S A SIMPLE ENOUGH PREMISE: Six pals sit around a coffee shop (or a rent-controlled Greenwich Village apartment), sipping espressos and dissecting their lives in minute detail, whether it be last night's disastrous date or a job interview gone wrong. Nothing in *Friends*' straightforward logline hinted at the massive worldwide hit it would become when it debuted on NBC in 1994, spawning catchphrases ("How *you* doin'?"), hairstyles (the Rachel) and at least one radio earworm (the Rembrandts' "I'll Be There for You"). Then again, there's no predicting the magical alchemy of sharp, clever writing and a cast brimming with chemistry and charm.

Created by David Crane and Marta Kauffman and originally titled *Insomnia Cafe*, the series was meant to capture that period in early adulthood when friends become second families. And as luck would have it, at the same time the creative team was pitching the pilot, NBC Entertainment president Warren Littlefield was looking for a show about twentysomethings to add to the network's lineup. Crane and Kauffman's treatment was a perfect fit. After a few more name changes (*Friends Like Us* to *Six of One* to, finally, just *Friends*), the sitcom hit the air, and the rest, as they say, is television history. *Friends* would become the cornerstone of NBC's Must See TV Thursday-night lineup, making stars of its leads (Jennifer Aniston, Courteney Cox, Lisa Kudrow, Matt LeBlanc, Matthew Perry and David Schwimmer) and running for 10 seasons. But perhaps the more surprising story isn't *Friends*' initial success but the long tail it's enjoyed since the finale's closing credits ran.

Friends first went into broadcast syndication (aka reruns) in 1998, meaning viewers no longer had to wait until Thursday to get their fix. In fact, throughout the early 2000s, it was pretty easy to find reruns on multiple channels throughout the day, and that continued after original episodes stopped airing. Then, in 2014, Netflix landed the streaming rights to the series, making all episodes viewable in one place, at one time, and in order (which, unless you owned the DVD collection—or slavishly recorded each episode on VHS—hadn't really been possible up to that point). This move introduced the series to a whole new generation of fans who seemed to revel in the show's simple delights.

Yet despite many of the sitcom's timeless themes, certain aspects have soured with age. Even in the '90s, *Friends*' lack of characters of color was noteworthy, and nearly 30 years on, that dearth is even more stark. (We are talking about a show set in New York City—the melting pot of America!) Then there's the fatphobic way in which Monica's weight struggles were handled and the misgendering of Chandler's trans parent. To their credit, the show's creators have acknowledged their mistakes and sought to make amends. In 2022, after coming to terms with the way she'd handled diversity on the show, Kauffman donated $4 million to her alma mater, Brandeis University in Waltham,

↑ Clockwise from left The cast celebrate Jennifer Aniston's win at the 2002 Emmy Awards; fans outside a Central Perk pop-up in London; a fan inside a Central Perk pop-up in New York; Perry's new memoir; *The Reunion.*

Mass., to establish an endowed professorship in the African and African American studies department. That same year, she also noted her regret over the use of incorrect pronouns for Chandler's parent.

"I've learned a lot in the last 20 years," Kauffman told the *Los Angeles Times*. "Admitting and accepting guilt is not easy.... I'm embarrassed that I didn't know better 25 years ago."

The ensuing decades have also allowed the stars time to reflect on their life-changing experiences. In 2021 the gang reunited (for only the second time since filming ended) on HBO Max's *Friends: The Reunion*, where they revealed secrets like clandestine intra-cast crushes and where they think their characters would be today. And fans felt the love: *Variety* reported that 29 percent of streaming households in the U.S. watched the special on release day. The following year Perry got even more candid about his time on the series (including his struggles with drug addiction) in his memoir *Friends, Lovers, and the Big Terrible Thing*, which became a *New York Times* No. 1 bestseller.

Through the highs and the lows, it's clear fans will never truly be done with Ross, Rachel, Chandler, Monica, Joey and Phoebe. And how could we be? These Friends are practically family. EW

MEET THE

From breakups and makeups to bad hair days and even worse

FRIENDS

first dates, these six were always in it together. *By Gina McIntyre*

The gang's first meeting was at the table read for the pilot—and their chemistry was nearly instant.

Monica Geller

COURTENEY COX

Perfectionist to the core, hyper-competitive New York chef Monica is the levelheaded hub around which the other friends orbit: Rachel is her long-lost best friend; Ross, her brother; Phoebe, her former roommate; and Joey and Chandler, her neighbors. She serves as a kind of den mother to the eclectic group, and her spotless apartment, which she's illegally subletting from her grandmother, is the place the gang most often gather—apart from Central Perk, of course. Fiercely loyal to the people she loves, Monica will definitely be there for you, you know, when the rain starts to pour.

Notably, Monica's maternal instinct was baked in to the character from the start. *Friends* co-creators David Crane and Marta Kauffman had also envisioned her as tough, cynical and sarcastic, and they'd offered the role to *Reality Bites* star Janeane Garofalo. Courteney Cox—then best known for her supporting turn on sitcom *Family Ties* and as the wide-eyed fan in Bruce Springsteen's "Dancing in the Dark" music video—they saw as Rachel. But Cox knew better. Feeling she could relate to Monica's goal-oriented, type A personality, she successfully lobbied the producers for the part.

And thankfully so. Cox always finds a way to make the most of Monica's quirks and contradictions—in her hands, Monica is genial, independent and understanding, at the same time she's dictatorial, neurotic and desperate to be liked. Regrettably, adult Monica's surfeit of confidence comes at least in part from no longer being the insecure, overweight girl she was in high school, something that's pointed out way too often. The "fat jokes" were never okay, but they sound especially troubling heard through today's ears.

↑ **From left** Monica's apartment (pictured), where the Friends often hang out, is always spotless; Rachel, before the iconic, much-copied haircut.

Rachel Green

JENNIFER ANISTON

The oldest child of a privileged Long Island family, spoiled ex-cheerleader/sorority girl/soap opera fan Rachel entered adulthood with no real idea of how to live on her own. After jilting fiancé Barry at the altar, the runaway bride headed straight to Manhattan to look up old pal Monica and found a whole new life waiting for her at Central Perk, one without the safety net of her father's credit cards. Soon she was living in Monica's second bedroom and waitressing at the coffeehouse to pay the rent, slowly forging a path toward independence—something her two younger sisters never did manage.

Although Jennifer Aniston had been on several sitcoms before she was cast on *Friends*, the role of Rachel rocketed her both to superstardom and

to the celebrity haircut hall of fame. Aniston's shoulder-length layered bob was dubbed the Rachel, inspiring countless copycat looks on women all around the globe. Maybe not surprising considering that, as a character, Bloomingdale's enthusiast Rachel always did have impeccable style—she hits her professional stride once she breaks into a career in fashion, eventually landing at Ralph Lauren.

If only her love life had been so straightforward. As *Friends* grew in popularity, the fate of Rachel's relationship with Ross became a national obsession: Would they get together? (Yes!) Would they stay together? (No!) Were they on a break? (Definitely! But maybe not?) Would they get back together? (Obviously! He's her lobster.) Although it took a while, they did get their happy ending, concluding the show as a couple, years after they'd already been raising daughter Emma together as, well, friends. Unconventional, sure, but romantic nonetheless.

Recurring Characters

COWORKERS, EXES AND EVEN AN EVIL TWIN.

By Gina McIntyre

Gunther

JAMES MICHAEL TYLER

So maybe he doesn't have a last name, but the Central Perk barista doesn't need one to make an outsize impression, serving up scones and carrying a massive torch for Rachel. With his bleached-blond hair and sarcastic demeanor, Gunther is a largely silent observer to the antics on the orange couch, but when the character does speak, Tyler (who died in 2021) always makes it count.

Jack and Judy Geller

ELLIOTT GOULD AND CHRISTINA PICKLES

A consistent, and consistently hilarious, presence on the series since its second episode, genial if clueless Jack and disapproving (of Monica) Judy make little effort to hide the fact that Ross is their favorite child. Says dad Jack early on: "I read about these women trying to have it all, and I thank God, our little Harmonica doesn't seem to have that problem."

RECURRING CHARACTERS

Janice Litman-Goralnik (née Hosenstein)

MAGGIE WHEELER

Oh. My. Gawd. Famous for her flamboyant fashion sense and loud, braying laugh, Janice is Chandler's on-again, off-again girlfriend. Delightfully confident and actually quite well-meaning, Janice never seems to understand just how much the gang dislike her—though she does resolve to win Joey over with "Joey and Janice's day of fun!" (It doesn't work.) Once she and Chandler finally call it quits, Janice still turns up at the most surprising or inopportune moments.

Carol Willick and Susan Bunch

ANITA BARONE/JANE SIBBETT & JESSICA HECHT

When *Friends* opens, Ross is reeling from the breakup of his marriage to college girlfriend Carol (played in one episode by Barone, with the role then going to Sibbett), who's recently come out as gay and is moving in with her partner, Susan, a woman she met at the gym. Only one episode later Ross learns Carol's pregnant with their son. Ross and acerbic Susan always maintain something of a jealous rivalry, but the trio still successfully co-parent young Ben.

Phoebe Buffay

LISA KUDROW

Gloriously unconventional, masseuse/folk singer Phoebe is the sexually adventurous free spirit whose deadpan honesty is delightfully refreshing ("I wish I could, but I don't want to" is seriously the best way ever to turn down an invite to put together furniture). The character easily could have tipped over into manic-pixie dream girl territory were it not for her surprisingly bleak origins: Her adoptive mother died by suicide, her father abandoned the family, her stepfather went to prison, and she ended up living on the streets at the age of 14. The fact that Phoebe's alive and thriving is a minor miracle.

So is the fact that Kudrow was cast in the role, which others like Jane Krakowski auditioned for. Although Crane and Kauffman loved Kudrow's take on the character, James Burrows, who was directing the *Friends* pilot, had just fired her from another landmark comedy, *Frasier*—she had been cast in that show as Roz,

but was later deemed wrong for the part. Kudrow did a second *Friends* audition for Burrows, winning him over. Once the comedy debuted, she won over audiences, too, and along with David Schwimmer, became the first cast member nominated for an Emmy.

Kudrow brought buoyancy, self-confidence and edge to her portrayal of the amateur songwriter ("Smelly Cat"). At almost every turn, Phoebe chooses to embrace optimism and relies on her tight-knit found family for love and support—even when she makes the most surprising choices. Like, say, carrying triplets as a surrogate for the half brother she didn't know she had or singing wildly inappropriate songs to school children or just running through the park with reckless abandon (whether Rachel likes it or not).

↖ **From left** Phoebe's a glass-half-full kind of gal despite a hard childhood; Ross's complicated love life becomes a running gag on the show.

Ross Geller

DAVID SCHWIMMER

The show's hopeless (or is that helpless?) romantic, Ross does not have great luck in the relationship department, though his rapport with pet monkey Marcel was pretty solid for a while there. But that's because the nerdy paleontologist is destined to be with the one woman he's loved since high school, Rachel. He says her name at the altar during his second wedding ceremony (to Emily), which ultimately leads, unsurprisingly to the second of his three divorces.

Although the role of Monica's older brother was written with David Schwimmer in mind—he and *Friends* executive producer Kevin Bright had previously worked together—bad experiences in television had soured the actor on the medium, and he had decided to pursue a theater career instead. Fortunately the creative team cajoled him into accepting the part: Who else could have possibly pulled off the Holiday Armadillo costume he wears to teach son Ben about Hanukkah?

Unquestionably sweet but extremely uncool, Ross has a knack for getting himself into countless awkward predicaments: moving his new couch upstairs ("Pivot!"); delivering lectures in a questionable British accent; whitening his teeth to a blinding degree; attempting to wear leather pants on a date. Yet no matter how absurd the situation, Schwimmer is always game, playing Ross as a fundamentally decent if goofy guy with a tendency toward both despair and rage. Still, it's the moments when Ross is at his most honest and vulnerable that resonate—like his stunned, stammering reaction hearing that Rachel has put the feelings she developed for him behind her. "You're, you're over me?" he asks hesitantly. "When... when were you... under me?" Heartwarming and hilarious.

Chandler Bing

MATTHEW PERRY

New York's most sarcastic statistical analysis and data reconfiguration professional (that's right, we know his job), Chandler Bing—or as he's known on his *TV Guide* label, Miss Chanandler Bong—sort of hates his corporate gig, though it does enable him to help finance roommate Joey's acting ambitions. Although Chandler often references his fear of commitment, he's deeply loyal to Joey and the other members of the gang, including future wife Monica.

Perry's friend Craig Bierko had initially been offered the part, but when Bierko chose to work on a different sitcom, Perry hurriedly auditioned for Chandler, who he felt mirrored his own personality. It was during those first performances that Perry invented the character's unique speech pattern, which became a signature quirk: "Could she BE more out of my league?" (And no, he wasn't talking about frequent girlfriend Janice.)

Although his behind-the-scenes struggles with substance abuse have been well documented, including in Perry's own memoir, the actor unfailingly delivered onscreen, rattling off a stream of witty asides and self-deprecating wise cracks. Like Monica, Chandler's insecurities stem from his childhood days, when his parents' divorce left him traumatized. And like Monica's backstory, Chandler's doesn't look great today, with his parent's transgender identity repeatedly played for laughs.

What is truly funny is Chandler's rapport with BFF Joey: their matching leather recliners—ideal for *Baywatch* viewing and their days jointly raising the chick and the duck. The pair proved inseparable to the end. When Chandler moves to the suburbs with Monica and their adopted twins, their new house has a special room just for Joey (no sex swings allowed).

↑ **From left** Chandler is the jokester of the group; Joey's acting career experiences many highs and lows, but he's always a hit with the ladies.

Joey Tribbiani

MATT LeBLANC

Delightfully dim-witted actor and onetime Al Pacino butt double, Joey is a man of simple pleasures—sex and sandwiches mostly, not always in that order. Fortunately his go-to pickup line, "How *you* doin'?" never fails, and his dating prospects are only bolstered once he lands the role of handsome neurosurgeon Dr. Drake Ramoray on *Days of Our Lives* (a much better gig than, say, starring in *Freud!*, the musical). But the brother to seven sisters is a fundamentally decent guy, which makes his incessant flirting so comically endearing rather than simply tiresome.

So much of Joey's undeniable charm came directly from Matt LeBlanc's approach to the

character, who had started out on paper as a more traditional lothario and was destined for a romantic future with Monica—the writers planned for the duo to become the show's central couple. The leading-man types who had been brought in to read for the part felt oddly bland, however. By contrast, LeBlanc's well-meaning himbo energy took Joey in a different, far more lighthearted direction, allowing him to blend in more seamlessly with the other members of the ensemble.

In contrast to tightly wound pals Ross and Chandler, Joey is easygoing and confident, even if he isn't the most intellectually gifted of his peers. Indeed, Joey's most head-scratching moments see LeBlanc at his best, like the time the refrigerator breaks, and Joey does the "sensible" thing and eats all the food inside. Or when Joey famously advises Rachel on her office crush: "If he doesn't like you, this is all a moo point.... Yeah, it's like a cow's opinion. It just doesn't matter. It's moo." EW

RECURRING CHARACTERS

Ursula Buffay
LISA KUDROW

The phrase "evil twin" never felt so apropos. Putting an original spin on a classic TV trope, Kudrow plays her own self-absorbed sister, Ursula, who's as wildly unconventional as Phoebe but lacks any sort of moral compass. (Kudrow actually played Ursula first, as a ditzy waitress on the sitcom *Mad About You*—after Kudrow won the part of Phoebe, the *Friends* writers decided it would be fun for the character to cross over.) Largely estranged, the siblings only have occasional—albeit memorable—run-ins.

Frank Buffay Jr.
GIOVANNI RIBISI

Phoebe and Ursula aren't the only Buffay children. Attempting to find the father who walked out on her, Phoebe instead meets her clueless half brother, whose hobbies include melting things and who wrongly assumes that Phoebe is a sex worker when he hears that she's a professional masseuse. Frank Jr. becomes a pivotal figure in Phoebe's life when he and his former home ec teacher/new wife Alice (Debra Jo Rupp) ask her to be their surrogate, and she ends up delivering triplets.

SEASON 1

Where It All Began

Get to know the six New York twentysomethings (plus one monkey!) navigating the ups and downs of love and life from the cozy confines of Central Perk

Runaway bride Rachel explains her plight to former schoolmates Monica and Ross and their friend Phoebe.

***FRIENDS* DEBUTED ON SEPT. 22, 1994, TO A LARGELY WARM** reception, with *EW*'s TV critic Ken Tucker writing in his A- review: "At its best, *Friends* operates like a first-rate Broadway farce, complete with slamming doors, twisty plots and intricately strung together jokes. And even when it's not at its best, the crack acting and piquant punch lines give *Friends* a momentum and charm that win you over even if you're not laughing."

1. The One Where Monica Gets a Roommate

PLOT We're introduced to the gang at Central Perk, where the Friends are having one of their many meandering chats (Chandler's naked anxiety dream) over lattes. Their personas are nailed before the first commercial break: Joey, the dim-bulb lothario actor; Monica, the fastidious singleton; Chandler, the self-deprecating wiseass; Phoebe, the New Age flake; Ross, the depressed divorcé whose wife has just ditched him for another woman; and rich girl Rachel, Monica's high school pal, who runs into Central Perk in a wedding dress having just left her husband-to-be, Barry, at the altar. Rachel moves in with Monica—even if it means being cut off from Daddy's dollars, prompting her new roomie to offer *Friends'* mission statement: "Welcome to the real world. It sucks! You're going to love it." **HISTORIC MOMENT** Rachel begins her stint as Central Perk's worst waitress. **BEST LINE** "Do the words 'Billy, Don't Be a Hero' mean anything to you?" (Ross, on how long it's been since he's had sex) **REVIEW** It's remarkable how quickly this ensemble establishes a comfortable, comedic vibe. After 22 minutes, these six people are believably set up as lifelong buddies. **B+**

2. The One With the Sonogram at the End

PLOT Monica's in a tizzy as she prepares for a visit from her self-esteem-sucking folks. Rachel gives Barry back his engagement ring—and learns he's now dating her maid of honor, Mindy. **INTRODUCES** Ross's ex-wife Carol (Anita Barone) and her girlfriend Susan (Jessica Hecht); Barry (Mitchell Whitfield); Elliott Gould and Christina Pickles as the Gellers. **HISTORIC MOMENTS** Ross finds out he's going to be a dad; first Ugly Naked Guy sighting; Gunther (James Michael Tyler) appears at Central Perk but has no lines; we learn Monica was once chubby, Chandler is an only child, and Phoebe is a twin, which explains Kudrow's continuing presence on *Mad About You*. **BEST LINE** "Oh, I think this is the episode of *Three's Company* where there's some kind of misunderstanding." (Chandler) **NEW DO** Joey **REVIEW** A snappy episode, packed with smart backstory—including Monica's perfectionist roots. Establishes the comedically fertile Ross-Susan-Carol triangle. **B+**

3. The One With the Thumb

PLOT Monica bemoans how the gang always picks apart her dates, but she's even more dismayed when they finally like one—waaaay more than she does. Meanwhile, ex-smoker Chandler gets rehooked. **BEST LINE** "Loosely translated, 'We should do this again' means 'You will never see me naked.'" (Monica) **REVIEW** Slow pacing and feeble secondary plots, but Phoebe gets ample screen time, allowing Kudrow to define her delightfully daffy character. **B**

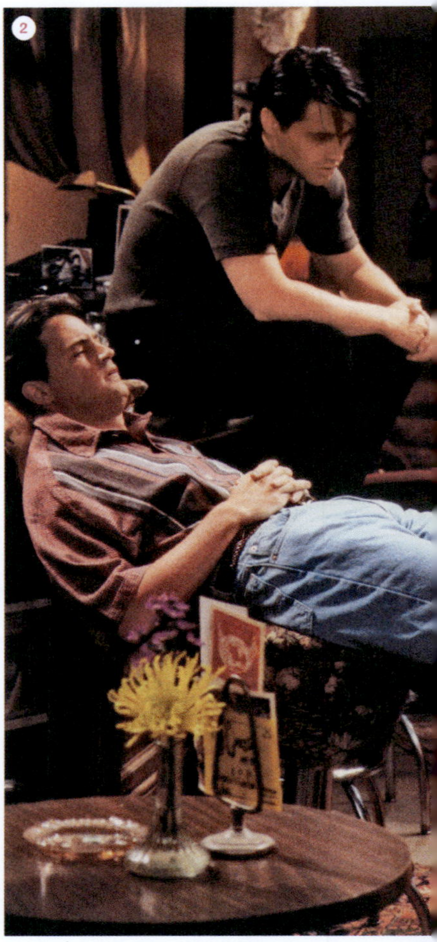

4. The One With George Stephanopoulos

PLOT Chandler and Joey bring Ross to a hockey game to take his mind off Carol—but a puck to the face doesn't help. The girls throw a slumber party and attempt to take Rachel's mind off being the only one of her hometown friends who isn't getting promoted, married or pregnant—and things really pick up when George Stephanopoulos's pizza is delivered to their pad by mistake. **BEST LINE** "I think you have to draw him out. And then, when you do, he's a preppy animal!" (Monica, speculating on Stephanopoulos's sexual prowess) **REVIEW** Kudrow, Cox and Aniston are effortlessly hilarious at the drunken slumber party,

but give the boys their props: Joey's confusion over the difference between omnipotent and impotent is a gut-buster. **A-**

2. Rachel takes a job waitressing at Central Perk. **3.** Monica gets dating advice from coworker Paula (Jenifer Lewis). **4.** The gang gets tied up in a game of Twister.

5. The One With the East German Laundry Detergent

PLOT Dumping is the theme of the day: Chandler dreads ending it with his heretofore unseen girlfriend—and it doesn't get any easier after multiple espressos; Joey enlists Monica to help him break up his ex-girlfriend and her new boyfriend. **INTRODUCES** Janice (Maggie Wheeler). **HISTORIC MOMENT** Rachel kisses Ross for the first time—as a token of appreciation for helping her do laundry. **BEST LINE** "You know what blows my mind? Women can see breasts anytime they want." (Joey) **REVIEW** Ross's unrequited love for Rachel emerges as the series' one ongoing story line, and their laundry date is the first time Aniston and Schwimmer show off their cute chemistry. **B+**

6. The One With the Butt

PLOT Chandler becomes the boy toy of a worldly Italian woman (Sofia Milos) who's already got a husband and a boyfriend, while Joey lands his first movie role—as Al Pacino's butt-double. Too bad he can't keep his derriere from overacting. **HISTORIC MOMENT** Joey gets an agent (Estelle Leonard Talent Agency). **CREATIVE CASTING** Series director James Burrows as the movie's director. **NEW DO** Rachel **BEST LINE** "After all your years of struggling, you've finally been able to crack your way into show business." (Chandler, to ass stand-in Joey) **REVIEW** LeBlanc's Joey started off as the cast's weakest link, but around this time in the series, he ditches Tribbiani's more clichéd aspects and displays deceptively subtle comic instincts. **A-**

7. The One With the Blackout

PLOT Manhattan is hit with a power outage, leaving Chandler trapped in an ATM vestibule with a model, the gang confessing sex secrets in Monica's candlelit pad and Ross attempting to escape "the friend zone" by asking Rachel out. **INTRODUCES** Paolo (Cosimo Fusco), Rachel's Italian beau;

Monica and Rachel's perpetually peeved downstairs neighbor Mr. Heckles (Larry Hankin). **CREATIVE CASTING** Jill Goodacre Connick as herself. **BEST LINE** "Who am I going to meet in a blackout? Power company guys? Eligible looters?" (Monica) **REVIEW** The series is at its best when plot contrivances are put aside for chatty, casual comedy mixed with physical high jinks (Ross wrestling Paolo's cat on the balcony is definitive *Friends* slapstick). **A-**

8. The One Where Nana Dies Twice

PLOT Ross and Monica mourn the passing of their grandmother—who doesn't quite make it into the light with her first attempt—but it's Ross who ends up six feet under. **BEST LINE** "So he's calling from Rome. I can do that. I just gotta go to Rome." (Ross, about Paolo) **REVIEW** *Friends* is atypically adept at handling schmaltz—e.g., babies and weddings—but the somewhat maudlin sentiment of Nana's death lands with a thud. **B-**

9. The One Where Underdog Gets Away

PLOT It's Thanksgiving, but nobody's feeling grateful when the gang get locked out of Monica's apartment after running outside to see an escaped Underdog balloon from the parade. **INTRODUCES** Jane Sibbett as the new Carol. **BEST LINE** Joey: "I have a question… I don't see any tater tots." Monica: "That's not a question." **REVIEW** While this is a holiday episode first and foremost, it's the subplot—new model Joey inadvertently becomes a clinic's poster boy for VD—that's truly worth celebrating. **B**

10. The One With the Monkey

PLOT The gang forgo New Year's Eve dates and have dinner together—but one by one they break their resolution. **INTRODUCES** Marcel the Monkey (see sidebar). **HISTORIC MOMENTS** Phoebe sings her first song in Central Perk. **CREATIVE CASTING** Hank Azaria as Phoebe's scientist boyfriend. **BEST LINE** "Hey, that monkey's got a Ross on his ass." (Chandler) **REVIEW** Introducing the monkey was perhaps *Friends*' biggest blunder—forcing Schwimmer to do comedy opposite a simian is beneath him. "Monkey" illustrates the writers' tendency to overplot, and the multiple story lines never quite jell. Still, any episode that gives Phoebe center stage gets bumped up a grade. **B**

11. The One With Mrs. Bing

Chandler's mom, a lusty and beautiful romance novelist, hits town—and hits on Ross. Phoebe and Monica make a love connection of their own: After they startle a cute guy with a catcall, he's hit by a car, leaving him in a coma and the girls fighting over nursemaid duties. **INTRODUCES** Morgan Fairchild as Chandler's mom. **BEST LINE**

Monkey Business

WHY DAVID SCHWIMMER WASN'T FRIENDS WITH HIS FURRY SCENE PARTNER.

By Amy Wilkinson

↑ Schwimmer and his simian sidekick in 1994.

Dr. Ross Geller may have had a sentimental attachment to his primate roommate Marcel, but actor David Schwimmer was hardly bananas about working with Monkey and Katie, the two female capuchins who shared the role.

"I hate the monkey," Schwimmer famously told *EW* back in 1995. "The trainers won't let me bond with it. They're really, really possessive. It's like, 'Land on your marks, do your job, don't touch or bond with the monkey.' It's a bummer."

At least the annoyance was short-lived: Marcel was written off the show by the end of season 1. Having reached his sexual maturity (i.e., humping everything in sight), Marcel was sent to live out his days in the San Diego Zoo. The character would make one more appearance during season 2's post-Super Bowl outing, filming *Outbreak 2: The Virus Takes Manhattan* with Jean-Claude Van Damme. (When Rachel asks how famous Marcel is, a crew member replies: "In human terms? I'd say Cybill Shepherd.")

In real life, Katie went on to nab a handful of roles post-*Friends*, including parts on *30 Rock* and *Sam & Cat*. (Sadly, trainer Mike Morris revealed in 2020 that Monkey had died of cancer.)

For Schwimmer, it seems time has not softened his perspective: When asked during HBO Max's *Friends: The Reunion* in 2021 what his least favorite part of filming was, Schwimmer replied, "The monkey."

7. Chandler gets stuck in an ATM vestibule with Jill Goodacre Connick. 8. Jack Geller (Elliott Gould) and his little Harmonica. 11. Morgan Fairchild makes her debut as Chandler's mom.

"You don't kiss your friend's mom. Sisters are okay, maybe a hot-lookin' aunt, but not a mom. Never a mom." (Joey, to Ross) **REVIEW** Jay Leno's appearance is a portent of the NBC crossovers to come. While Mr. and Mrs. Geller brilliantly inform the Ross and Monica characters, the idea that Chandler's mom is a bawdy sexpot is confusing. Add the forced Coma Guy story line and you have the weakest *Friends* outing yet. **C**

12. The One With the Dozen Lasagnas

PLOT Ross prepares for the birth of Carol's baby—though he can't decide if he wants to know the sex; Phoebe prepares to tell Rachel that Paolo made a pass at her. **HISTORIC MOMENTS** We see Phoebe at work as a massage therapist; Joey and Chandler buy a foosball table; and it's official—Ross's baby is a boy! **BEST LINE** "We are way past the fling thing. I mean, I am feeling things that I've only read about in Danielle Steel books." (Rachel, on Paolo) **REVIEW** Masterfully silly cold open—the gang humming the *Odd Couple* theme in Central Perk—sets the tone for this meandering, somewhat scattered but charming installment. **B+**

13. The One With the Boobies

PLOT It was bound to happen with all this barging in and out of one another's apartments: Chandler walks in on a half naked Rachel. Joey meets his dad's longtime mistress. **INTRODUCES** Joey's dad, Joey Sr. (Robert Costanzo), and his mom, Gloria (Brenda Vaccaro). **CREATIVE CASTING** Fisher Stevens as Phoebe's psychiatrist beau Roger. **NEW DO** Monica **BEST LINE** "If I turn into my parents, I'll either be an alcoholic blond chasing after 20-year-old boys or—I'll end up like my mom." (Chandler) **REVIEW** The parent-child role reversal of the Joey story line is tired, but the show does a hilarious job of mocking its Gen X hipness with Roger's denunciation of the gang's "codependent, emotionally stunted" dynamic. **B**

14. The One With the Candy Hearts

PLOT It's Valentine's Day, and the gang is dealing with dating disasters: Chandler's blind date turns out to be his ex Janice; the girls nearly torch Monica's apartment with an out-of-control "boyfriend bonfire"; poor Ross ends up sharing a table with his ex-wife while on a date. **BEST LINE** "C'mon, man—she's needy. She's vulnerable. I'm thinking, 'Cha-ching!'" (Joey) **REVIEW** What *Friends* does best is mine laughs from love woes. Janice and Chandler's anti-chemistry continues to yield shrill comedy, and the bonfire is just the kind of true-to-life silliness we love. **B+**

15. The One With the Stoned Guy

PLOT After five years of data processing, Chandler heads to a career counselor—and learns he's ideally suited for...data processing. Monica tries to land a head chef position but is chagrined when the restaurateur attends her tasting stoned. Ross dates the curator of insects at his museum, but bugs out when she wants him to talk dirty. **CREATIVE CASTING** Jon Lovitz as the pothead. **REVIEW** Lovitz's stoner shtick is an unfunny stunt-casting gimmick, but the episode is redeemed by an all-time classic scene in which Joey teaches Ross to talk dirty. resulting in this **BEST LINE** "If you can't talk dirty to me, how are you going to talk dirty to her? Now, tell me you want to caress my butt!" **A-**

16. The One With Two Parts

PLOT Joey falls for Ursula, Phoebe's bitchy identical twin—continuing Ursula's habit of stealing all of her sister's stuff. Ross goes to Lamaze class with both Carol and Susan. **CREATIVE CASTING** First in a series of Must-See TV crossovers: *Mad About You*'s Helen Hunt and Leila Kenzle drop by Central Perk and mistake Phoebe for Ursula. **BEST LINE** "It's mostly just like dumb sister stuff, you know. I mean, like, everyone always thought of her as the pretty one." (Phoebe on Ursula) **REVIEW** Flights of fancy do not suit this sitcom, and this installment is full of them—including Rachel dangling off the balcony tangled in Christmas lights. One redeeming factor: the subtle sweetheart dynamic between Joey and Phoebe. **C+**

17. The One With Two Parts—Part 2

PLOT The high jinks continue as an injured and uninsured Rachel needles Monica into defrauding the hospital by letting Rachel use her insurance. **CREATIVE CASTING** It's another NBC crossover: *ER*'s George Clooney and Noah Wyle play two M.D.'s whom Monica and Rachel date. **HISTORIC MOMENT** Phoebe and Joey kiss! (He thinks she's Ursula.) **BEST LINE** Rachel: "I use my breasts to get other peoples attention." Monica: "We both do that." (Each speaking as the other) **REVIEW** Far superior to the pallid Part 1, thanks to Monica and Rachel's wickedly funny insurance-fraud-necessitated identity swap. Still, the gooey Marcel-in-peril ending is unforgivable schmaltz. **B**

↓ **BEST EPISODE**

18. The One With All the Poker

PLOT The girls try to beat the guys at poker, while Ross keeps bluffing about his feelings for Rachel. **BEST LINE** "Hello, Kettle? This is Monica. You're black." (Phoebe, when Monica calls Ross "competitive") **REVIEW** Besides being rife with genius Chandler comebacks (Rachel: "Guess what?" Chandler: "Uh, okay—the fifth dentist caved, and now they're all recommending Trident?"), "Poker" proves the power of this ensemble; the six players spend almost the entire 22 minutes together, and it's the best episode so far. **A**

19. The One Where Marcel Gets Away

PLOT Rachel loses Marcel, throwing a monkey wrench into Ross's plan to confess his true feelings for her. **BEST LINE** "What happened to 'Forget relationships! I'm done with men!'—the whole, uh, penis embargo?" (Ross, to Rachel) **REVIEW** The nadir of *Friends'* first-season simian-centric plots, chock-full of pointless monkeying around, including a random Shaft gag that culminates with Phoebe getting shot in the butt with a tranquilizer gun. Oh, the hilarity! **C**

20. The One With the Evil Orthodontist

PLOT Rachel reconnects with Barry—even though he's engaged to her friend Mindy. Chandler sends himself into a stress spiral when a girl doesn't call him after "one of the greatest first dates of all time." **NEW DO** Rachel **CREATIVE CASTING** *Dirty Dancing* star Jennifer Grey as Mindy. **BEST LINE** A cold open for the ages. Chandler: "I can't believe you would actually say that. I would much rather be Mr. Peanut than Mr. Salty." Joey: "No way. Mr. Salty is a sailor, all right? He's gotta be, like, the toughest snack there is." **REVIEW** Aniston's a whiz at milking Rachel's high-strung guilt for laughs, but did we ever believe Rachel would end up with Barry when millions of viewers are rooting for Ross? **B**

21. The One With the Fake Monica

PLOT After Monica's credit card is stolen, she tracks down the thief and becomes enamored of the Fake Monica's free-spirited ways. **HISTORIC MOMENT** Ross sends Marcel to a zoo. **BEST LINE** "Let's just say my Curious George doll is no longer curious."(Rachel, after an amorous Marcel attacks her stuffed animal) **REVIEW** A thin, hokey episode with a semi-sappy "carpe diem" theme. And that "Marcel likes to hump things" joke isn't getting any funnier the zillionth time around. **C**

15. Jon Lovitz guest-stars as a stoned restaurateur. **16.** *Mad About You* characters Fran (Leila Kenzle) and Jamie (Helen Hunt) mistake Phoebe for her twin, Ursula. **23.** Ross welcomes son Ben with Joey and Monica. **24.** Rachel dreams about what a romance with Ross could be like.

22. The One With the Ick Factor

PLOT Monica is dating "young Ethan" (Stan Kirsch) but doesn't find out how young he is until after she sleeps with him. Chandler discovers his entire staff hates him when he hires Phoebe as his temp secretary. **BEST LINE** "Oh God, I just had sex with someone who wasn't alive during the Bicentennial!" (Monica) **NEW DO** Chandler **REVIEW** A perfectly balanced episode: Monica's hysterics over her boyfriend are countered by Chandler's chagrin over being "Bossman Bing." **A-**

23. The One With the Birth

PLOT Carol goes into labor, but Ross and Susan's constant bickering gets them tossed out of the room—and eventually locked in a storage closet. **CREATIVE CASTING** Leah Remini as a single mom; June Gable (later cast as Estelle, Joey's agent) as a nurse. **BEST LINE** "I love them—each one's like a little party in my uterus!" (Carol, after the doctor asks how she's doing with the contractions) **REVIEW** Once again, *Friends* delivers standard-issue sitcom devices (the locked-in-a-closet gag; tearjerker ending) with charm and restraint. Schwimmer works his nebbishy anxiety to great effect, while Phoebe reminds us that she's actually the most insightful Friend with a sweet observation of Susan and Ross: "Here's this little baby who has, like, three whole parents who care about it so much they're fighting over who gets to love it the most." Dammit—we told ourselves we wouldn't cry. **A-**

24. The One Where Rachel Finds Out

PLOT Rachel discovers Ross's love for her when Chandler lets it slip at her birthday party. Meanwhile, Ross is in China, where he digs up a new fossil—and a new girlfriend. **INTRODUCES** Julie (Lauren Tom), Ross's new squeeze. **BEST LINE** "Wow, you're going to be making money hand over fist." (Phoebe, learning what Joey will earn for his sperm donations) **REVIEW** Though the long awaited Ross-'n'-Rachel romantic revelation is ostensibly the focus, we found ourselves more entertained by the B-story: Joey's got a new girlfriend, but he's also participating in a fertility study that requires celibacy. There's nothing like sex jokes to temper shmoopy sitcom sentimentality. **B** EW

SEASON 2

Love Is in the Air

Audiences can't get enough of the will-they-won't-they romance between Ross and Rachel—and their devotion is finally rewarded as the couple get together

Lovebirds Ross and Rachel interrupt Joey and Chandler's TV time.

TALK ABOUT MUST-SEE TV: THE series notched its highest overall ratings in season 2 while marking another milestone: a post-Super Bowl episode that brought out all the stars (hello, Julia Roberts!).

1. Rachel meets Ross's new girlfriend Julie (Lauren Tom). **2.** The girls admire Ross's infant son when Susan (Jessica Hecht) and Carol (Jane Sibbett) stop by. **6.** Joey and Chandler experience adventures in babysitting. **7.** Ross and Rachel finally share their first real kiss.

1. The One With Ross's New Girlfriend

PLOT Rachel's big plan to reveal her love for Ross at the airport crashes and burns when he arrives on the arm of fellow paleontologist Julie. **NEW DO** Joey, Chandler **BEST LINE** "Okay, you have to stop the Q-tip when there's resistance!" (Chandler, to Joey) **REVIEW** An exquisite story (Rachel's vexation at losing Ross before she even had him) and inspired subplot (Phoebe mixes up her Moores and gives Monica Dudley's, not Demi's, do) start the sophomore season on a high note. **A-**

2. The One With the Breast Milk

PLOT Ross is thrilled when his sister befriends Julie, but Monica is guilt-ridden for betraying Rachel. The gang dare Ross to taste Carol's breast milk. **NEW DO** Monica **BEST LINE** "You're going to Bloomingdale's with Julie? It's like cheating on Rachel in her house of worship." (Chandler, to Monica) **REVIEW** *Friends* is best at finding the funny in relationship quandaries, e.g., Monica's confession to Rachel of her friendship infidelity ("I was thinking of you the whole time!"), so we'll forgive the occasional lame sitcommery—like Joey's "showdown" with a fellow cologne spritzer at Saks. **B+**

3. The One Where Heckles Dies

PLOT Cranky Mr. Heckles gets posthumous revenge on noisy neighbors Monica and Rachel by willing them an apartment's worth of junk. Chandler is horrified to discover that the lonely Heckles is him in 30 years. **HISTORIC MOMENT** Janice pops up pregnant and married. **BEST LINE** "Monkeys, Darwin—you know, it's a nice story. I just think it's a little too easy." (Phoebe, on why evolution is a crock) **REVIEW** It's good to see the boys' quirks under the microscope: Besides Chandler's meltdown over being mayor of "Bitter Town," Phoebe calls Ross on his obsessive need to be right. **A-**

4. The One With Phoebe's Husband

PLOT Phoebe's got a secret: She married her gay Canadian friend Duncan because he needed a green card. Oh, and Chandler has a third nipple. **HISTORIC MOMENT** Ross reveals that he's been with only one woman in his life—Carol. **CREATIVE CASTING** Steve Zahn as Duncan. **BEST LINE** "Oh, darn it—we're all out of milk. Hey, Chandler, will you fill me up here?" (Ross, holding a pitcher up to Chandler's chest) **REVIEW** Poor Phoebe's string of dead-end loves continues. And is it just us, or is Rachel's attempt to break up Ross and Julie a little nasty? **B**

Giovanni Ribisi, who will later play Phoebe's half brother, as a guy who drops a condom in her guitar case. **BEST LINE** "I don't think we brought enough stuff. Did you forget to pack the baby's anvil?" (Chandler) **REVIEW** NBC's philosophy must go something like this: If a hit show ain't broke, jam it with stunts and crossovers. Still, LeBlanc, Perry and Kudrow manage to turn those contrivances into unexpected hilarity. **B+**

↓ **BEST EPISODE**

7. The One Where Ross Finds Out

PLOT During Rachel's latest dating disaster, she insists she's totally over Ross—which is exactly what she tells him in a drunken phone message. Meanwhile, Monica is channeling her out-of-work energy into whipping Chandler into shape as his personal trainer. **HISTORIC MOMENT** Ross and Rachel's first real kiss. **BEST LINE** "You're over me?... When...when were you...under me?" (Ross, to Rachel) **REVIEW** This one never gets old: Aniston exhibits an endearing willingness to look foolish (see Rachel's wine-soaked blind date and next-day remorse) and gives her most Emmy-worthy performance yet. She and Schwimmer bring off Ross and Rachel's Central Perk blowout with sweet, silly perfection. **A**

5. The One With Five Steaks and an Eggplant

PLOT Joey, Phoebe and Rachel are nonplussed when Chandler expects them to pony up $62 for Ross' b-day gift, and they accuse their more gainfully employed pals of being insensitive to their money woes. **HISTORIC MOMENT** Monica gets fired for accepting free steaks from the meat vendor. **BEST LINE** "Um, is, is there any chance that you're rounding up, from, you know, like from, like $20?" (Phoebe, on the tab for Ross' birthday) **REVIEW** At long last, *Friends* shatters the fantasy that twentysomething New Yorkers with minimum-wage jobs can afford spacious apartments and $200 haircuts. It's also a rare—and welcome—treat to see the gang experience realistic tension. **B+**

6. The One With the Baby on the Bus

PLOT Joey and Chandler are left in charge of baby Ben and use him as bait to meet women—but end up leaving the tot on the bus. **HISTORIC MOMENT** Phoebe's "Smelly Cat" debuts. **CREATIVE CASTING** Lea Thompson, as *Caroline in the City*'s Caroline, who mistakes Joey and Chandler for a gay couple; Chrissie Hynde as Stephanie, Phoebe's "professional" Central Perk replacement;

8. The One With the List

PLOT Ross must choose between fulfilling his 10-year fantasy with Rachel and staying with Julie, so he composes a "pros and cons" list. Do we really need to tell you that Rachel finds the list? Monica is hired to develop recipes for Mockolate, a "completely synthetic chocolate substitute." **CREATIVE CASTING** Michael McKean as the Mockolate exec. **BEST LINE** "Oh, sweet Lord—this

A Cut Above the Rest

HOW 'THE RACHEL' BECAME THE MUST-HAVE LOOK OF THE '90S.

By Amy Wilkinson

In the season 1 episode "The One With the Evil Orthodontist," Rachel (Jennifer Aniston) debuted a new shorter do—choppy face-framing layers that hit right at the shoulders. The cut was dreamed up by celebrity hairstylist Chris McMillan (who has since admitted he was high when he did it), and neither he nor Aniston had any idea of the phenomenon it would inspire. Dubbed the Rachel, the cut would become one of the most copied of all time, in league with Farrah Fawcett's shag or Dorothy Hamill's wedge. At the time, New York hairdresser Rodney Cutler told *EW* that more than half of his clients were requesting it. Despite its popularity, Aniston wasn't a fan, later telling *Allure* in 2011: "I think it was the ugliest haircut I've ever seen." Which is probably why in season 3 she started growing it out. But she may never fully escape the Rachel: Thanks to the HBO Max reunion, the cut has experienced something of a resurgence—albeit modernized for the 2020s.

is what evil must taste like!" (Phoebe, sampling Mockolate-chip cookies) **REVIEW** Ross's list is an old TV gimmick—an artificial obstacle designed to keep a happy couple apart—but it's also a clever example of how boys can be so damn stupid. Still, after the giddy high of the Kiss, this episode comes off as a downer. **B**

9. The One With Phoebe's Dad

PLOT Phoebe learns that nothing her mother told her about her absentee father (he's a famous tree surgeon who lives in a phoneless hut in Burma) is true. Turns out Frank Buffay is a pharmacist in upstate New York—so Phoebe enlists Chandler and Joey for a road trip. A broken radiator turns Monica's holiday get-together into a "tropical Christmas party." **HISTORIC MOMENTS** Gunther speaks! We see Phoebe's apartment with her grandma. **CREATIVE CASTING** *Three's Company*'s Audra Lindley as Phoebe's grandma. **BEST LINE** "Ho ho ho holy crap, is it hot in here." (Chandler) **REVIEW** It's nice to finally get a real glimpse into Phoebe's tragicomic past, and Kudrow tempers the plot's poignancy with her award-winning daffiness. **B**

10. The One With Russ

PLOT Everybody but Rachel can see that her new boyfriend, Russ (Schwimmer, under a bad wig and a ton of makeup), is just a bigger-chinned doppelgänger for Ross. **INTRODUCES** Joey's agent Estelle (June Gable). **HISTORIC MOMENTS** Joey lands the role of Dr. Drake Ramoray on *Days of Our Lives*. **BEST LINE** "See, now they're as different as night and…later that night."(Monica, comparing Ross and Russ) **REVIEW** And we thought the Phoebe/Ursula gag was hackneyed. When a show as superior as *Friends* starts wandering into *Brady Bunch* territory (everybody remember when Peter met his twin at school?), it is a sad, sad day indeed. **C-**

11. The One With the Lesbian Wedding

PLOT Ross is shaken up when Carol and Susan announce their impending nuptials; Rachel is shaken up by a visit from her mom—especially when she learns that her parents might separate; **INTRODUCES** Marlo Thomas as Sandra Green. **BEST LINE** "Why wouldn't I want to come? I had fun at the first wedding." (Ross, to Carol) **REVIEW** A slightly overcrowded episode; still, Thomas is parent-perfect casting as Rachel's bubbly socialite mom, and Kudrow somehow makes a goofy poltergeist plot work. **B**

12-13. The One After the Super Bowl, Parts 1 & 2

PLOT *Friends*' second hour-long episode is a Hollywood drop-in extravaganza: *Days* doc Joey dates his first stalker (Brooke Shields); Phoebe falls for a library employee (Chris Isaak); the gang visit Marcel—now a monkey thespian—on the set of *Outbreak 2*, while Rachel and Monica fight over the movie's star, Jean-Claude Van Damme (guesting as himself); Chandler takes up with a fourth-grade classmate (Julia Roberts) who's still steamed about an undies prank he pulled. **HISTORIC MOMENT** Shields's frenetic performance as the soap fan led to a TV deal—which in turn led to *Suddenly Susan*. **CREATIVE CASTING** In addition to the above, Fred Willard as the administrator of the zoo where Marcel was last seen; *The Simpsons*' Dan Castellaneta as the zookeeper. **BEST LINE** "There will be times when you get older when you'll want to sleep with people just to make them

like you, but don't!/ 'Cuz that's another thing that you don't want to do. Everybody!" (Phoebe, in a song for a children's program) **REVIEW** Coinciding with the height of *Friends* hysteria (and a Diet Coke tie-in), "TOATSB" shows that the writers felt the pressure of producing a megahit: The episode is fragmented, poorly paced and only sporadically funny. Cramming the ensemble with celebs may have been a ratings grabber (52.9 million fans tuned in), but the results are forced sitcomedy and stilted acting (that means you, Mr. Van Damme). Roberts comes off the best (no surprise), though her offscreen mini-romance with Perry was more entertaining. **C**

14. The One With the Prom Video

PLOT Rachel has a message for Ross: "We are never going to happen, okay?" But she hasn't seen the titular video, which shows the geeky genesis of Ross's undying

12. Brooke Shields plays an obsessed fan pining over Joey's Dr. Drake Ramoray. **13.** Rachel rubs elbows with action star Jean-Claude Van Damme. **15.** Monica begins a romance with her parents' friend Dr. Richard Burke (Tom Selleck).

love. Joey, rolling in soap opera dough, repays Chandler for years of mooching with a gold bracelet, which his chagrined pal dubs an "eyesore from the Liberace house of crap." **HISTORIC MOMENTS** Our first glimpse of teenage Rachel's pre-nose job honker and of Fat Monica. (Cox in a fat suit has not aged well.) **BEST LINE** "See? He's her lobster!" (Phoebe, on Ross and Rachel) **REVIEW** So nice to see you again, director James Burrows. Putting the flashy guest stars and monkey high jinks behind it, "TOWTPV" brings the show back to relatable relationship comedy. The prom vid is witty character development disguised as a standard flashback. **A**

15. The One Where Ross and Rachel... You Know

PLOT It's Ross and Rachel's first date, but their journey from friends to lovers is hampered by Rachel's giggles and Ross's hectic schedule. **INTRODUCES** Dr. Richard Burke (Tom Selleck) as a Geller family friend. **HISTORIC MOMENT** Joey and Chandler acquire black leather armchairs. **BEST LINE** "I can't believe two cows made the ultimate sacrifice so that you guys could watch TV with your feet up." (Phoebe, about the new chairs) **REVIEW** Schwimmer and Aniston are almost too good at portraying the awkward buddies-to-bedmates transition (perhaps owing to their real-life crushes on one another); it's a little disconcerting seeing Ross and Rachel finally getting busy. But the latest champions in the chemistry department are Cox and Selleck. **B+**

16. The One Where Joey Moves Out

PLOT Joey and Chandler's blissful cohabitation ends when a *Days* star offers Joey his posh pad. Mr. and Mrs. Geller learn Richard is dating a twentysomething "twinkie," and they're shocked to discover it's their little Harmonica. **BEST LINE** "It's not like we

17. Chandler doesn't exactly find a soulmate in new roommate Eddie (Adam Goldberg). **20.** Joey and Chandler are back to their old shenanigans. **21.** Monica (in a blonde wig and glasses) performs for the patrons at the '50s-themed diner where she works. **22.** Rachel's mom (Marlo Thomas) comes for a visit. **23.** Instead of a romantic weekend, Phoebe and her sailor boyfriend (Charlie Sheen) contract chicken pox.

agreed to live together forever. We're not Bert and Ernie." (Joey, to Chandler) **REVIEW** Yep, the dissolution of TV's cutest couple is a shame, but it's a stellar drop-in from the older Gellers that makes this episode a success. **B+**

17. The One Where Eddie Moves In

PLOT A lonely Chandler takes in new roomie Eddie. Monica tries not to lose it now that Ross is hanging out at her pad 24/7 because of his blossoming relationship with Rachel. **HISTORIC MOMENT** Joey and Chandler's fave show, *Baywatch,* makes its first appearance. **INTRODUCES** Adam Goldberg as Eddie. **BEST LINE** "Hey, nice pillow. So now tell me, is this genuine Muppet skin?" (Rachel, on Joey's new decor) **REVIEW** Chandler and Joey's "breakup"—and the resulting tension over "rebound roommate" Eddie—is a pitch-perfect relationship parody. It's also nice to see Ross and Monica act like a bickering brother and sister for a change. **A-**

18. The One Where Dr. Ramoray Dies

PLOT Joey mouths off to *Soap Opera Digest* about scripting his lines on *Days,* so the writers put an empty elevator shaft in Dr. Drake's future. Chandler discovers the unbalanced side of Eddie. **HISTORIC MOMENT** Richard tells Monica he loves her. **BEST LINE** "This game is grotesque! Twenty armless guys joined at the waist by a steel bar, forced to play soccer forever? Ugh, hello—human rights violation!" (Phoebe, on foosball) **REVIEW** A pair of standout moments: Eddie's freakishly funny retelling of his recent breakup and Monica and Rachel's to-the-wire negotiations over the apartment's last condom. **B**

19. The One Where Eddie Won't Go

PLOT Joey faces the harsh reality of unemployment, while the girls get fired up by the feminist book *Be Your Own Wind-Keeper*. And Eddie won't move out. **HISTORIC MOMENTS** We learn Gunther used to play Bryce on *All My Children*; Joey moves back in with Chandler. **BEST LINE** "Joey, you owe $1,100 at I Love Lucite."

(Ross, surveying Joey's oversize Visa bill) **REVIEW** The *Wind-Keeper* plot is a smart send-up of New Age jibber-jabber—and the gals are gamely "I Am Woman"—but the feminism-as-punchline theme is a tad disturbing. The saving grace is guest star Goldberg's twitchy turn as Eddie. **B**

20. The One Where Old Yeller Dies

PLOT Phoebe goes on a quest to see the sad movie endings her mom shielded her from; Ross freaks out Rachel by revealing his plans for their future. **HISTORIC MOMENT** Ross and Rachel say the L-word. **BEST LINE** "Okay, what kind of a sick doggie snuff film is this?" (Phoebe, at Yeller's tragic conclusion) **REVIEW** Kudrow steals another show with Phoebe's cinema-fueled disillusionment: "It should've been called *It's a Sucky Life and Just When You Think It Can't Suck Anymore, It Does!*" **A-**

21. The One With the Bullies

PLOT When Ross and Chandler get to Central Perk, there are two mean guys on the couch who won't budge. Phoebe makes another attempt to meet her real dad; a broke Monica gets a job at a '50s-themed diner. **INTRODUCES** Giovanni Ribisi (seen in episode 6) as Phoebe's long-lost half brother Frank Buffay Jr. **BEST LINE** "I was a sous chef at Cafe des Artistes. How can I take a job where I have to make something called Laverne and Curly fries?" (Monica) **REVIEW** An atypically slapsticky episode, but it works. The final diner scene with Monica dancing to "YMCA" while wearing flame-retardant boobs is a howler. **A-**

22. The One With Two Parties

PLOT Monica is forced to split Rachel's birthday soiree between apartments to keep the divorcing Greens apart. **INTRODUCES** Ron Leibman as Rachel's abrasive dad, Dr. Leonard Green. **BEST LINE** "I start miles beneath the surface of these things." (Monica, on her uniform) **REVIEW** Chandler's reaction to the wacky premise ("Think—what would Jack and Chrissy do?") says it all—this episode is pure *Three's Company*, from the hyperphysical comedy to the Jack Tripper-Mr. Roper dynamic between Ross and Dr. Green. But the high-energy shenanigans don't quite mesh with the melancholy divorce theme. **B-**

23. The One With the Chicken Pox

PLOT Phoebe's Navy submarine officer boyfriend resurfaces—but her hopes for a romantic interlude are torpedoed when they both contract chicken pox. Joey creates an alter ego, the irritatingly successful family man "Joseph," for his new job at Chandler's company. **CREATIVE CASTING** Charlie Sheen as Phoebe's sailor. **BEST LINE** "You know, I might have expected this of you, Phoebe, but, Ryan, you're a Military Man!" (Ross barging in on the two scratching each other) **REVIEW** A forced setup combined with an out-of-place guest star (the pre-*Spin City* Sheen was clearly still uncomfortable with TV) equals one disappointing episode. It's notable only for a pair of dirty-by-*Friends*-standards one-liners in the cold open, including "That'll teach you to lick my muffin!" **C**

24. The One With Barry & Mindy's Wedding

PLOT Rachel's duties as maid of honor at her ex-fiancé's wedding are made all the more distasteful by her pouffy pink bridesmaid's dress. And Chandler's online love interest turns out to be a lady from his past. (We'll give you a hint: Oh. My. Gawd.) **HISTORIC MOMENT** Monica and Richard come to an impasse over children—she wants 'em, he doesn't. **CREATIVE CASTING** Jennifer Grey must've been busy, because Mindy is played here by Jana Marie Hupp. **BEST LINE** "I'm sorry, we don't have your sheep." (Chandler, seeing Rachel in her bridesmaid's getup) **REVIEW** A leisurely paced season-ender with plenty of sharp one-liners, "TOWBAMW" is given emotional heft by Richard and Monica's heartrending split—a bittersweet scene that allows Cox and Selleck one last chance (for now) to show off their superb chemistry. **A-** EW

SEASON 3

Battle of the Sexes

It's not just the Geller Cup placing our guys and gals at odds: When Rachel lands a new job at Bloomingdale's (and a hunky new colleague), she and Ross end up on a break

Monica, Phoebe and Rachel do everything they can to stop Joey from scoring a touchdown.

BY SEASON 3, *FRIENDS* HAD REALLY HIT ITS STRIDE, DELIVERING SOME of the series' most memorable episodes, including "The One Where No One's Ready," "The One With the Football," and, of course, "The One Where Ross & Rachel Take a Break."

1. The One With the Princess Leia Fantasy

PLOT Monica is still mourning her breakup with Richard; Ross and Rachel act out his Carrie Fisher gold-bikini fantasy from *Return of the Jedi*. **BEST LINE** "This guy's so stupid. It's Count Rushmore!" (Joey, watching *Wheel of Fortune*) **NEW DO** Chandler, Joey **REVIEW** The Princess Leia bit is a perfect example of the writers spinning a plot out of a pop-culture touchstone, and Ross's discovery that "women tell each other everything" is a relatable, comedically rich concept. But Monica's bummery-ness is a bummer. **B+**

↓ **BEST EPISODE**

2. The One Where No One's Ready

PLOT Ross is the only one dressed a half hour before a museum fundraiser. Monica gets a "call me" message from Richard on her machine. **BEST LINE** "I'm not gonna go commando in another man's fatigues." (Joey, on why he has to wear underwear with a rented tux) **REVIEW** The episode plays out in a single room, in real time, with just the six Friends, and it deftly leans into each character's personality quirks (see: neurotic Monica leaving multiple messages on Richard's machine, including the declaration: "I'm breezy!"). And Joey wearing all of Chandler's clothes? One of the all-time great sitcom sight gags. **A**

2. Joey wears all of Chandler's clothes.
3. Joey consoles Monica.
5. Ross meets one of his celebrity crushes, Isabella Rossellini.
6. In a flashback episode we learn Chandler tried to pick up an engaged Rachel.

3. The One With the Jam

PLOT Monica tries to get over Richard by throwing herself into jam-making, then decides she wants to have a baby on her own—and discovers Joey's been making deposits at a sperm bank. Phoebe falls for Malcolm, her twin's stalker, but dumps him because he's still obsessed with Ursula. **CREATIVE CASTING** David Arquette (the future Mr. Courteney Cox) as Malcolm. **BEST LINE** "Pheebs, wake up and smell the restraining order." (Chandler) **REVIEW** Monica's yearning for a child adds a new emotional layer to her post-Richard recovery. It's one of Cox's best performances. **B**

4. The One With the Metaphorical Tunnel

PLOT Phoebe poses as Joey's agent, but her brutal honesty about why he's being rejected drives him back to Estelle. Ross is distressed to see his son playing with a Barbie doll. Chandler decides to "go through the tunnel" and make a commitment to Janice. **BEST LINE** "So he plays with a Barbie? Big deal. You used to dress up like a woman." (Monica, to Ross) **NEW DO** Monica **REVIEW** Phoebe's fake-agent routine is a riot, and so is Chandler's attempt to settle down with Janice. Sensitive Ross's concern over his son's masculinity seems out of character—until we learn about his past. Still, it's hard to see this plotline making the cut in 2023. **B**

5. The One With Frank Jr.

PLOT Phoebe reunites with her brother Frank Jr. The gang discuss who'd be on their "freebie list"—five stars they'd be allowed to sleep with and not jeopardize their relationships. Ross puts Isabella Rossellini on his, then removes her—only to bump into the star at Central Perk. **CREATIVE CASTING** Isabella Rossellini as herself. **BEST LINE** "She's too political—she probably wouldn't do it unless you donated four cans of food first." (Chandler, on why Susan Sarandon, who later guests on the show, wouldn't be on his list) **REVIEW** The "freebie list" is a brilliant concept that had viewers constructing their own. And Giovanni Ribisi is an excellent addition. **B+**

6. The One With the Flashback

PLOT Janice asks if the Friends have ever almost hooked up, prompting a flashback to three years earlier, when Chandler is searching for a roommate (enter Joey) and putting the moves on Rachel (who's getting cold feet over her impending marriage). Ross, having learned his wife is gay, makes out on a pool table with Phoebe, who is secretly moving out of Monica's apartment. **BEST LINE** "This actor guy, who I'm not sure about because when he called and I answered the phone 'Chandler Bing,' he said 'Whoa, short message.' (Chandler, on potential new roommate Joey) **NEW DO** Ross, Joey, Chandler, Rachel **REVIEW** Often a corny conceit, the flashback is again used well here to allow us a peek at what the gang was like right before the series began. The romantic tension that develops between Joey and Monica is even funnier now that we know she ends up with Chandler. **A-**

7. The One With the Race Car Bed

PLOT Ross dreads a dinner with Rachel's impatient doctor dad, who calls him "Wethead." Joey goes with Monica to return a race-car bed wrongly delivered by the Mattress King, aka Janice's ex, and sees her cheating on her "Bing-aling." **BEST LINE** "If I squint, I can pretend he's Alan Alda." (Rachel, on the supersensitive Ross) **REVIEW** The car bed seems a random object on which to hang an episode, but Janice's reunion with her ex is a shocker. **B**

8. The One With the Poking Device

PLOT Joey tells Chandler he caught Janice with her ex-husband. Ross doesn't trust Rachel to babysit Ben, but it's Monica who bumps the tot's head. **BEST LINE** "It serves me right for buying a 12-pack of condoms." (Chandler, after his breakup with Janice) **REVIEW** The two-women-and-a-baby physical shtick with Monica and Rachel

12. Ross is not a fan of Rachel's new coworker Mark. **13.** Monica and Richard reunite. **14.** Phoebe tries to make beautiful music again with Leslie.

works surprisingly well, but the one-liners fall flat. And while Chandler's split with Janice was inevitable, she'll be missed. **B-**

9. The One With the Football

PLOT Some Thanksgiving touch football reawakens the sibling rivalry between Ross and Monica. **HISTORIC MOMENT** We learn of the Geller Bowl and the Geller Cup—a troll doll nailed to a two-by-four that Mr. Geller supposedly threw in the lake but Monica actually saved. **BEST LINE** "Nice try. See, the Netherlands is this make-believe place where Peter Pan and Tinkerbell come from." (Joey) **REVIEW** Set on a not-very-convincing soundstage, this episode is a bit predictable (Monica and Ross are hyper-competitive, Rachel's not great at football), yet a winning entry in the Thanksgiving episode canon. **B**

10. The One Where Rachel Quits

PLOT Just before Christmas, Gunther tells Rachel she needs to be retrained as a waitress, and she quits. After landing a job at Fortunata Fashion, she finds herself making coffee again. Monica gets hooked on Mint Treasures. **BEST LINE** "Well, as old as he is in dog years, do you think Snoopy should still be allowed to fly this thing?" (Chandler) **REVIEW** It's nice to see Gunther speak more than his usual one or two lines and a good idea to get Rachel out of working at Central Perk. But there's nothing more depressing than watching a Christmas episode in any month other than December. **C+**

11. The One Where Chandler Can't Remember Which Sister

PLOT A tipsy Chandler hooks up with one of Joey's sisters. Rachel meets Mark, who helps her get a job at Bloomingdale's. **INTRODUCES** Steven Eckholdt as Mark. **BEST LINE** "You do not wanna tick her off. She was, like, the sixth person to spit on Mussolini's hanging body." (Joey, on his grandmother) **REVIEW** This episode titillatingly pushes the sexual envelope (there's even talk of a threesome Joey once had). And watching Chandler try to figure out which sister he fooled around with plays to Perry's strengths (befuddlement being one of them). **B+**

12. The One With All the Jealousy

PLOT Ross gets jealous when Mark takes Rachel to lunch. Monica hooks up with Julio, a hunky coworker at the diner, only to discover his contempt for American women. Joey auditions for *A Tale of Two Cities*, not realizing the role requires dance experience, which he doesn't have. **BEST LINE** "Everybody lies on their résumés—I wasn't one of the *Zoom* kids either." (Joey) **REVIEW** The script sheds insight on male-female dynamics, as Chandler and Joey explain how Mark is positioning himself to become Rachel's confidant before making his move. And speaking of moves, Joey's dance scenes are a kick. **B+**

13. The One Where Monica and Richard Are Friends

PLOT Monica runs into Richard at the video store. Phoebe's new boyfriend Robert has a habit of hanging out of his shorts (as Chandler discovers, to his horror). **BEST LINE** "Hey, buddy, this is a family place—put the mouse back in the house." (Gunther, alerting Robert to his exposure) **REVIEW** The guys' reaction to Robert's unintentional exhibitionism is sidesplitting (they decide not to look directly at it—"like an eclipse"). **B**

14. The One With Phoebe's Ex-Partner

PLOT Phoebe reunites with former musical collaborator Leslie, but the duo have a falling out over "Smelly Cat." Chandler meets Joey's ex Ginger, whose artificial leg Joey accidentally burned. Mark leaves his job at Bloomie's but plans to go to a lecture with Rachel. **HISTORIC MOMENT** Chandler undergoes a "nubbinectomy" to remove his third nipple. **CREATIVE CASTING** Elizabeth "E.G." Daily (*Rugrats*) as Leslie, and Sherilyn Fenn (*Twin Peaks*) as Ginger. **BEST LINE** "When we were playing together, that was the most fun I ever had in, like, all my lives." (Phoebe, discussing Leslie) **REVIEW** The wooden-leg plotline is tasteless. At least the tension between Ross and Rachel sets the stage for their impending breakup. **C**

15. The One Where Ross & Rachel Take a Break

PLOT After Rachel tells Ross she has to cancel their anniversary plans, he surprises her at the office. Later she tells him they need to "take a break." He winds up sleeping with Chloe, the hottie from the copy store. **HISTORIC MOMENT** Duh—Ross and Rachel break up. **BEST LINE** "You do not bring a picnic basket to somebody's work—unless maybe they're a park ranger." (Rachel, to Ross) **REVIEW** There's real emotional resonance to Ross and Rachel's split. At the same time, the episode lays the groundwork for one of the series' funniest mantras: "We were on a break!" **A**

16. The One With the Morning After

PLOT Ross frantically tries to keep Rachel from finding out he's slept with Chloe, but Gunther spills the beans. **BEST LINE** "What were you trying to put it in—her purse?" (Rachel, after Ross says his sleeping with Chloe was a "mistake") **REVIEW** Schwimmer and Aniston have never been more heartbreakingly believable. Just as they're breaking up, they cement their status as one of TV's greatest couples. **A-**

17. The One Without the Ski Trip

PLOT Rachel invites everyone but Ross skiing, but when Phoebe's cab runs out of gas, who else are they gonna call? Meanwhile, Chandler takes up smoking again. **BEST LINE** "I can handle it—handle's my middle name. Actually, it's the middle part of my first name." (Chandler) **REVIEW** Ross and Rachel's breakup means a new dynamic among the sextet, but the temporary change of locale

Were They Really on a Break?

PONDERING THAT AGE-OLD QUESTION SPARKED BY SEASON 3'S CLASSIC EPISODE. *By Amy Wilkinson*

More than 25 years later, fans are still divided over whether Rachel and Ross were really, truly on a break when Ross decided slept with the copy girl Chloe (Angela Featherstone). Just how much has this ongoing debate burrowed its way into the cultural consciousness? Well, on Etsy you can actually purchase a doormat reading "Were Ross & Rachel on a break?" with the answers "Yes" and "No" printed below, allowing packages to be left on the deliverer's answer of choice. So, yeah, that's how much.

For the show's stars, however, the answer is pretty clear: When asked by James Corden during their HBO Max reunion special whether it was okay that Ross got together with Chloe, they all agreed it was because—you guessed it!—Ross and Rachel were on a break. So if Jennifer Aniston has made peace with it, perhaps the rest of us should too.

↑ Ross attempts to salvage his relationship with Rachel.

(most of the episode is set at a rest stop where they're stranded) takes the show out of its element (and not in a good way). Plus, a plot about Perry battling an addiction doesn't seem so funny in light of later real-life events. **C+**

18. The One With the Hypnosis Tape

PLOT Chandler uses a hypnosis tape to quit smoking, but it's geared toward women and starts changing his behavior in other ways. Frank Jr. announces he's getting married to his home ec teacher, Mrs. Knight. Pete, a millionaire Monica doesn't find attractive, takes her out for an Italian dinner—in Rome. **INTRODUCES** A pre-Marvel Jon Favreau as Pete; Debra Jo Rupp (*That '70s Show*) as Frank Jr.'s fiancée/schoolteacher. **BEST LINE** "Monica, last Saturday night, what happened on *Walker, Texas Ranger*?" (Rachel, proving to Monica she has no social life) **REVIEW** Frank Jr.'s back—yay! And Rupp brings a mature touch to her role, plus it's nice to see Monica finally get her groove back after Richard. **A-**

19. The One With the Tiny T-Shirt

PLOT Mark confesses his crush to Rachel and asks her out. Monica goes on another date with Pete. Joey lands a lead in an Off Broadway play opposite the sexy but contemptuous Kate. Rachel begins dating, and she and Ross return each other's stuff (including the title's tee). **INTRODUCES** Dina Meyer (*Starship Troopers*) as Kate. **BEST LINE** "I know I'm no Jon Bon Jovi. Or someone you find attractive." (Pete, to Monica) **REVIEW** Ross's reaction to Rachel's first post-breakup date is uproariously realistic, and when he gives his Frankie Goes to Hollywood T-shirt to her as a peace offering, it's undeniably affecting. **B+**

20. The One With the Dollhouse

PLOT Monica inherits her aunt Sylvia's dollhouse; Rachel's insensitive boss expresses interest in Chandler; Joey has a fling with Kate's understudy, which spurs Kate to sleep with him. **INTRODUCES** Alison La Placa as Rachel's boss. **BEST LINE** "I'm not interested in her sweater. It's what's underneath her sweater that counts." (Joey, to Kate, about her wool-clad understudy) **REVIEW** The guest cast just keeps getting stronger with the addition of La Placa, but the dollhouse stuff is kinda cloying. **B**

21. The One With a Chick and a Duck

PLOT Moping over Kate, Joey finds solace with a new chick—a real baby chicken. Chandler tries to dump the chick at a shelter but winds up bringing home a duck. Pete buys a restaurant and wants Monica to be its head chef. **BEST LINE** "Do you guys know how to get a chick out of a VCR?" (a panicked Chandler, running into Rachel's apartment) **NEW DO** Chandler **REVIEW** It's hard not to quack up at the duck-and-chick gags—especially when Joey and Chandler have a fight over who's spending more time with them. The Pete-Monica subplot gets a new life, extending the huggable Favreau's stay. **B+**

22. The One With the Screamer

PLOT Rachel's new boyfriend Tommy turns out to have a raging temper but only shows it in front of Ross. Joey consoles Kate after a bad review. **CREATIVE CASTING** Ben Stiller as Tommy; Peter Bonerz (Dr. Jerry Robinson from *The Bob Newhart Show* and the episode's director) as a theater patron. **BEST LINE** "I always have to pick the smartest guy or the most talented guy. Why couldn't I just pick someone like you?" (Kate, to Joey) **REVIEW** Stiller's a scream—he may be *Friends*' funniest guest star ever. Between Stiller, Jon Favreau, Dina Meyer and June Gable (as Joey's chain-smoking agent Estelle), this is the rare episode with a supporting roster as talented as its regulars. **A**

23. The One With Ross's Thing

PLOT Ross finds a growth on his lower back and goes to see Phoebe's herbalist. Pheebs juggles two guys, a firefighter and a teacher, who don't know about each other. Monica becomes convinced that Pete is preparing to propose, but

19. Ross—in a tight T—tries to make peace with Rachel. **21.** Chandler and Joey become parents—to a duck and a chicken. **22.** Rachel's new boyfriend Tommy (Ben Stiller) has got quite the temper, which only Ross seems to know. **24.** Pete (Jon Favreau) tries to live out his dream of being the Ultimate Fighting Champion as a dismayed Monica watches on. **25.** Phoebe finally meets her birth mother Phoebe (Teri Garr).

what he really tells her is that he wants to become…the Ultimate Fighting Champion? **CREATIVE CASTING** Kevin McDonald (*Kids in the Hall*) as Guru Saj. **BEST LINE** "What do you know? You married a lesbian!" (Rachel, after Ross offers Monica marital advice) **REVIEW** Neither of Phoebe's beaux is given enough screen time to do anything particularly interesting. But Rachel's overexcited reaction to Monica's presumed wedding wins laughs, as does Ross's paranoia about his health. **B**

24. The One With the Ultimate Fighting Champion

PLOT Pete gets whupped in his Ultimate Fighting match but refuses to quit. Chandler is mortified when his new boss slaps his butt. Phoebe asks Rachel if she can set Ross up with her friend Bonnie, who used to be bald. **INTRODUCES** Sam McMurray (*The Tracey Ullman Show*) as Chandler's boss; Christine Taylor (*The Brady Bunch Movie*) as Bonnie. **CREATIVE CASTING** Robin Williams and Billy Crystal crowd the gang on the couch at Central Perk. **BEST LINE** "I don't understand guys. I would never congratulate Monica on a great stew by, you know, grabbing her boob." (Rachel, about bottom-smacking) **REVIEW** Williams and Crystal's cameo is short-lived, and the episode only goes up from there, thanks to Chandler's inspired efforts to avoid his touchy-feely boss. **B+**

25. The One at the Beach

PLOT Phoebe and Co. head to the beach in Montauk, N.Y., so she can meet an old friend of her mother's, also named Phoebe, who makes a startling revelation. During the trip, Rachel tricks Bonnie into shaving her head again—a complete turnoff to Ross. **HISTORIC MOMENT** Chandler tells Monica, "If worst comes to worst, I'll be your boyfriend." She tells him that he's not boyfriend material. She'll soon change her tune… **INTRODUCES** Teri Garr as Phoebe's biological mom, Phoebe Sr. **BEST LINE** "C'mon, Daddy needs a new pair of electromagnetic microscopes for the prehistoric forensics department." (Ross, rolling the dice during a strip *Happy Days* board game) **NEW DO** Chandler **REVIEW** Garr's casting is genius. Rachel's trick on Bonnie is almost as entertaining as Ross's horrified reaction ("You can feel all the bones in your skull!"). And it's great to see Ross and Rachel kissing again. **A** EW

SEASON 4

Joey, Chandler, Rachel and Monica compete for huge stakes.

Big Changes

Rachel and Monica lose their apartment to Chandler and Joey during a quiz game. Meanwhile, Phoebe agrees to be her brother's surrogate, and Ross meets a new lady

IN ITS FOURTH SEASON, *FRIENDS* FINALLY NOTCHED ITS FIRST ACTING Emmy win: Outstanding Supporting Actress for Lisa Kudrow, whose real-life pregnancy was written into the show.

1. The One With the Jellyfish

PLOT The gang wind up their summer in Montauk. Ross dumps Bonnie after canoodling with Rachel, who later hands him an 18-page letter he falls asleep reading. The next morning she asks him simply, "Does it?" He takes a chance, saying it does...then finds that "It does" means he'll take responsibility for everything that went wrong with their relationship. Chandler provides some unconventional first aid to Monica's jellyfish sting... he pees on it. **BEST LINE** "And, hey, just so you know, it's not that common, it doesn't happen to every guy and it *is* a big deal! (Rachel, to Ross) **REVIEW** A solid, if not spectacular, beginning to what may be the series' strongest season. **A-**

2. The One With the Cat

PLOT A stray feline bounds into Central Perk, and Phoebe decides it's the reincarnation of her mom, Lily. Monica's elated to be asked out by Chip Matthews, the big man on her high school campus. While trying to sell his entertainment center, Joey is locked inside while the "buyer" robs his apartment. **BEST LINE** Monica: "Oh my God. Do you still live with your parents?" Chip: "Yeah. But I can stay out as late as I want." **REVIEW** Cox is swell bringing to life Monica's reenactment and vindication of her adolescence, while Perry and LeBlanc continue to hone their Abbott and Costello-esque jiving. **A-**

3. The One With the 'Cuffs

PLOT Chandler is sleeping with Rachel's boss, Joanna, who leaves him handcuffed and pantless in her office. Mrs. Geller bets that her daughter will "pull a Monica" while catering her party. She's right. **BEST LINE** "You must have me confused with 'The Amazing Chandler'!" (Chandler, unable to get out of the cuffs) **CREATIVE CASTING** Penn Jillette (of Penn & Teller) as an encyclopedia salesman. **REVIEW** Here's a theory: As Perry and Aniston go, so goes the show. In "'Cuffs" they're a frenzied physical riot. **A**

4. The One With the Ballroom Dancing

PLOT The building's huffy superintendent, Mr. Treeger, threatens to evict the illegally subletting girls...unless Joey helps him polish his rug-cutting skills in preparation for a formal dance. Phoebe gets hot and bothered over a hunky massage regular. **HISTORIC MOMENT** Phoebe is fired after she and said client are caught making out. **BEST LINE** "Oh, yeah, I'm a gym member. I try to go four times a week, but I've missed the last...twelve hundred times." (Chandler, trying to quit the gym) **REVIEW** LeBlanc and Mike Hagerty (as the super) elevate their scenario from merely silly to downright cute. **B+**

5. The One With Joey's New Girlfriend

PLOT Chandler falls for Kathy, Joey's new flame. Ross and Rachel try to stoke each other's jealousy with their new squeezes, but it turns out they're really just babysitting: he literally; she figuratively, with an undergrad doofus. **INTRODUCES** Paget Brewster as Kathy. **BEST LINE** "Who wants to make some long distance calls?" (Ross, learning his "date" is a babysitting gig) **REVIEW** Perry shines, both in the early scene where the gang tease him about his crush, and in his dash to say hello to Kathy. **B+**

6. The One With the Dirty Girl

PLOT Ross dates Cheryl, an extremely hot—and slovenly—paleontology doctoral candidate. Chandler buys Kathy a birthday gift (an early edition of her favorite childhood book, *The Velveteen Rabbit*) but allows Joey to claim it as his own when he makes a boneheaded purchase (a pen that's also a clock!). **HISTORIC MOMENT** Monica and Phoebe become

catering partners. **CREATIVE CASTING** Actually, we're going to call supermodel Rebecca Romijn's sweeps-month appearance as Cheryl uncreative casting. **BEST LINE** "Did Homo erectus hunt with wooden tools?" (Ross, after Cheryl asks him whether he wants to come in, post-date) **REVIEW** Ross's loose-limbed revulsion at Cheryl's untidy habits is almost as sublime as Chandler's O. Henry-worthy self-sacrifice. Nice editing in the post-funeral song-and-dance scene too. **A-**

1. Monica gets stung by a jellyfish, and Chandler takes matters into his own hands. **5.** Ross isn't too happy with Rachel. **7.** Chandler's got a thing for Joey's girl Kathy. **8.** Phoebe, Joey, Ross and Rachel chat with Chandler in a box.

7. The One Where Chandler Crosses the Line

PLOT Kathy becomes aware of Chandler's feelings for her and lets him know they're mutual. After the two impulsively make out, Chandler's got some 'splaining to do. Ross, with Phoebe's encouragement—and everyone else's aversion—takes to the keyboard to debut his "sound." **HISTORIC MOMENT** Guilt-ridden Chandler refurnishes the boys' apartment, complete with dual recliners and a new Foosball table. **BEST LINE** "I can't believe I ever let him touch me with those fingers." (Rachel, after hearing Ross's playing) **REVIEW** Ross's musical stylings provide yet another peek into his weirdo geek alienation, while Phoebe's awe at his "talent" seems perfectly appropriate. It's a nice giddy sideshow to the near-operatic arc that's developed around Joey and Chandler. **A-**

8. The One With Chandler in a Box

PLOT As punishment for betraying Joey (and inspired by Joey's entertainment-center imprisonment a few episodes ago), Chandler spends Thanksgiving in a carton in Monica's living room. Monica injures her eye poking around in the freezer and winds up consulting—and briefly dating—Richard's doctor son. **CREATIVE CASTING** *Never Been Kissed*'s Michael Vartan as Dr. Burke. **BEST LINE** "You can't tell, but I'm trying to break the tension by mooning you guys." (A box-bound Chandler) **REVIEW** The first truly great Turkey Day episode. Stellar performances all around, though Perry, despite spending most of the episode inside a box, steals the show. **A**

9. The One Where They Are Going to Party

PLOT The legendary Mike "Gandalf" Ganderson ("only, like, the funnest guy in the world," according to Ross) is coming to town to lead the boys on a bacchanalian adventure...but he gets stuck in Chicago, so they go it alone. Joanna promises to support Rachel in her pursuit of a promotion, then cuts her down in front of the hiring panel. Monica's scathing review of a local restaurant gets her hired as its chef. **BEST LINE** Explaining the origin of Ganderson's nickname, Ross says: "Didn't you read *Lord of the Rings* in high school?" Joey: "No, I had sex in high school." **REVIEW** "Party" is pleasantly lightweight, notable for the post-party scene in which the boys, having stopped trying to recapture their up-all-night youth, are the most mature we've seen them to date. Bummer to lose Alison La Placa's Joanna; her comic possibilities were endless. **B+**

↓ The *Friends* stars with the Rembrandts' Danny Wilde and Phil Solem.

About That Theme Song

'I'LL BE THERE FOR YOU' MADE THE REMBRANDTS A HOUSEHOLD NAME—AND A ONE-HIT WONDER.

By Rob Brunner

No one told them it was going to be this way. When Rembrandts partners Danny Wilde and Phil Solem were asked to record the *Friends* theme song, they figured it might be good for a giggle. "We were like, 'Wouldn't it be fun to hear ourselves on the TV?'" Wilde told *EW* in 2001. "'No one will ever know it's us.'" Yeah, right. With its catchy chorus and signature handclaps, the ditty jumped out of TV sets. Written by Michael Skloff with lyrics by Allee Willis, the tune was conceived as a duet for Michael Stipe and Natalie Merchant, who declined. Then the producers stumbled onto a little-known band called the Rembrandts. "They had almost a Lennon-McCartney kind of harmonization," Skloff said. The song took off, and the duo eventually recorded a three-minute version that spent eight weeks atop the *Billboard* airplay chart. The Rembrandts' mainstream success was ultimately short-lived: They broke up in 1997 but have reunited on and off to record new music. "I know we have people [at our shows] ... who care about us.... That song—I'm not ashamed of it. It put us on the map," Wilde said.

10. The One With the Girl From Poughkeepsie

PLOT Lonely at holiday time, Rachel allows Chandler to set her up with someone at his office. Monica faces a resentful kitchen staff, most of whom are related to her predecessor (fired as a result of her); she decides to hire, then fire, Joey to show them who's boss. **BEST LINE** "How can she be great if she's from Poughkeepsie? That joke would've killed in Albany." (Chandler) **REVIEW** The eponymous subplot—a run-ragged Ross dates both an unfunny uptown woman and a cute, funny Poughkeepsie girl—is a laugh loser. **B-**

11. The One With Phoebe's Uterus

PLOT No sooner do Frank Jr. and Alice tie the knot than they ask Phoebe if she'll carry their baby for them; Phoebe Sr. advises her to think twice and, as a cautionary lesson, gives her a puppy to take care of. Ross gets Joey a job as a tour guide at the museum. **HISTORIC MOMENT** The climactic museum-lunchroom scene, in which Ross orates against seating segregation, features not one but two Black characters! **BEST LINE** Phoebe: "I'm gonna be giving someone the greatest gift you can possibly give." Chandler: "You're gonna carry their child and get them a Sony PlayStation?" **REVIEW** "Uterus" commences the

Phoebe-as-mom arc (created to accommodate Kudrow's real-life pregnancy), but it's Rachel, Monica and Chandler who provide the episode's real comic nuggets—as when the girls educate an anxious Chandler about female erogenous zones. **B+**

11. Frank Jr. (Giovanni Ribisi) and wife Alice (Debra Jo Rupp) ask Phoebe to be their surrogate. **12.** Chandler and Joey (and their hideous dog statue) swap apartments with Monica and Rachel. **13.** Rachel has the hots for her personal shopping client Joshua (Tate Donovan).

↓ **BEST EPISODE**

12. The One With the Embryos

PLOT Joey's observation that laundry day means Monica is wearing old-lady undies sets off a who-knows-who-better battle between the boys and the girls. If the girls win, the boys get rid of the chick and duck; if the boys win, they get Mon's big purple apartment. Phoebe undergoes implantation of Alice's embryos. **HISTORIC MOMENTS** Chandler and Joey win the girls' pad; by way of Ross's high-stakes trivia questions, we learn scads of arcane information about the Friends. **BEST LINE** "He's a transponster!" (Rachel, wildly—and incorrectly—guessing Chandler's job) **REVIEW** Thanks to the trivia contest alone, "Embryos" is quite possibly *Friends'* finest moment. **A+**

13. The One With Rachel's Crush

PLOT Kathy's steamy, half naked appearance in a play has got Chandler worried about her offstage fidelity; Rachel is transferred to the personal-shopping department, where she clumsily tries to act on her feelings for Joshua, a newly divorced client. **INTRODUCES** Mr. Waltham (Paxton Whitehead), Rachel's stuffy new boss; onetime Aniston beau Tate Donovan as Joshua. **BEST LINE** "Why don't you call me when you grow up?" (Kathy, weary of Chandler's obsessive suspicion) Chandler: "Yeah, well, don't expect that to happen anytime soon!" **REVIEW** The hits just keep on coming for the Job-like Chandler, as his worst fear becomes a self-fulfilling prophecy. Also the beginning of a primo Rachel plot—her hapless pursuit of Joshua—elicits sheer brilliance from Aniston. **B+**

14. The One With Joey's Dirty Day

PLOT Joey returns from a fishing trip a little, um, fragrant, which earns him a misguided pep talk from his costar Charlton Heston. A double-booked Rachel asks Ross to take out Mr. Waltham's niece Emily from England. Monica and Phoebe try to help Chandler through the stages of breakup grief. **INTRODUCES** British actress Helen Baxendale as Emily. **BEST LINE** Phoebe, consoling Rachel: "Aw, Pheebes." Rachel: "Honey, that's your name." Phoebe: "That's short for Phoebe? I thought that was just what we called each other." **CREATIVE CASTING** Heston, whose conversation with Joey about actors "stinking" is a real beaut. **REVIEW** "Dirty Day" gives everyone something funny and/or meaningful to do and, with the arrival of Emily, gets the season's climactic arc started. **B+**

15. The One With All the Rugby

PLOT Ross meets a couple of rugby-playing buddies of Emily's and feels compelled to prove his mettle. Chandler has a chance meeting and date with the nails-on-blackboard Janice, who's now divorced. **BEST LINE** I'm riding the alimony pony! (Janice) **REVIEW** More physical fun from Schwimmer, who's always good for some yuks when Ross's masculinity is challenged. Monica, with her electric-switch obsession, is once again stuck with an extremely minor plotline. Perry and Maggie Wheeler's chemistry makes their generally strained story work. **B**

16. The One With the Fake Party

PLOT When pregnant vegetarian Phoebe is tortured by a craving for meat, Joey offers to trade dietary preferences with her. After learning that Joshua isn't ready to date, Rachel is determined to invite him to an as-yet-unplanned bon voyage party for Emily. **HISTORIC MOMENT** Phoebe eats meat! **BEST LINE** "I say more dumb things before 9 a.m. than most people say all day." (Chandler) **REVIEW** While a stunning group effort, "Fake Party" is dominated by Aniston, who in 22 wardrobe-changing, tooth-cracking, rib-tickling minutes delivers another tour de force that should have been enough to snag her an Emmy. Alas, it didn't. **A-**

17. The One With the Free Porn

PLOT Joey and Chandler happen upon an unscrambled "adult" cable channel and decide they'd better not shut off the set lest they lose it. Phoebe learns she's having triplets. **HISTORIC MOMENT** Ross tells Emily he loves her...and she says, "Thank you." **BEST LINE** "I was just at the bank, and there was this really hot teller, and she didn't ask me to do it with her in the vault!" (The porn-immersed Chandler) **REVIEW** As comedy formulas go, Joey + Chandler + free smut = a laugh riot. **B+**

18. The One With Rachel's New Dress

PLOT Ross gets homophobic (literally) when Emily hits it off with Susan, Carol's wife, and agrees to show her around London on her upcoming holiday. Joshua's folks arrive home prematurely from their vacation to find a skimpily clad Rachel in their home. Frank Jr. and Alice decide they want Phoebe to name one of the babies. **HISTORIC MOMENT** Phoebe announces that one of the triplets will be named Chandler. **CREATIVE CASTING** John Bennett Perry (Matthew's dad) as Joshua's dad. **BEST LINE** "I don't know about 'Hulk,' but I like the idea of a name starting with 'The'!" (Phoebe mulling baby names) **REVIEW** Aside from Joey and Chandler's child-like vying to be the namesake of Phoebe's kid-to-be, the light, transitional "Dress" seems designed mostly to scoot the show's current romantic relationships toward the finale. **B-**

19. The One With All the Haste

PLOT After Rachel is irked one too many times by the singing neighbor across the courtyard, the battle to reswap apartments is on. Ross can't stand the thought of Emily leaving and decides to do something about it. **HISTORIC MOMENTS** Ross and Emily get engaged, and the girls take back their pad. **BEST LINE** "What, we don't make enough fun of you already?" (Joey to Ross, who's sporting a new earring) **REVIEW** Funny how often *Friends* uses

20

lesbianism as a comic device. This time, the prospect of a 60-second Monica and Rachel sapphic kiss is enough to make Chandler and Joey give back the girls' pad. Although there is a positive in the bizarrely entertaining kicker: Joey's "Morning's Here" duet with the crooning neighbor. **B**

20. The One With All the Wedding Dresses

PLOT The girls are afflicted with wedding envy: Rachel blurts out an impromptu proposal to Joshua, while Monica and Phoebe take to hanging around the house in full matrimonial regalia. **BEST LINE** Monica: "This isn't even my dress!" Phoebe: "Well, at least you didn't rent yours from a store called It's Not Too Late." **REVIEW** For once this season, Cox—with some able support from Kudrow—is allowed

20. Phoebe and Monica go wedding crazy. **23.** In London, Chandler and Joey chat with a hat and scarf vendor played by business tycoon Richard Branson. **24.** Ross and Emily (Helen Baxendale) don't exactly have the smoothest nuptials.

to steal the show; her obsessive marital fascination is a thing of comic beauty. **B**

21. The One With the Invitations

PLOT Emily's by-the-by musing as to the wisdom of inviting exes to one's wedding has Ross (and us) waxing nostalgic with flashbacks of his and Rachel's history. **REVIEW** The dreaded clip show is usually filler designed to give a show's cast and crew a week off. Nevertheless, "Invitations" is still a bittersweet homage that gives the series' most resonant relationship its due. **B**

22. The One With the Worst Best Man Ever

PLOT Phoebe's mood swings have her careening from simpering damsel to seething bitch, leaving Monica and Rachel walking on eggshells. Ross's best man—Joey—orchestrates a bachelor party complete with souvenir T-shirts, a hot stripper...and a missing wedding ring. **BEST LINE** "It's not kicking me. It's kicking one of the other babies. Don't make me come in there!" (Pregnant Phoebe) **REVIEW** Okay, we forgave the clip show, but this water-treading half hour seems just plain lazy. **C**

23-24. The One With Ross's Wedding, Parts 1 & 2

PLOT The gang—minus a pregnant Phoebe and a heartbroken Rachel—head across the pond for Ross and Emily's "I dos." **HISTORIC MOMENT** Aside from the obvious, there's Chandler and Monica's wedding-eve hookup, a sweet narrative bookend to the flirty sparring and therapeutic peeing they shared in the season opener. **CREATIVE CASTING** This Anglo-palooza of stunt casting boasts a slew of cheeky cameos (Richard Branson, Hugh Laurie, June Whitfield, Olivia Williams, Fergie) as well as two howling turns from Tom Conti and *Absolutely Fabulous*'s Jennifer Saunders as Emily's parents, the Walthams. **BEST LINE** "London, baby!" (Joey) **REVIEW** Aching and sidesplitting, "Wedding" is a near-perfect finale that finds everyone at the top of their game (ironically, Kudrow's best work of the season is phoned in, literally, with Phoebe trying to get word to her pals that Rachel's en route to the nuptials). It's also got primo guest stars, a tantalizing cliff-hanger, and, in Chandler and Monica, a relationship that will have reverberations for seasons to come. **A** EW

SEASON 5

Chandler and Monica share a clandestine kiss.

More Than Friends

Perpetually single Chandler and Monica find their perfect matches in each other. Yet it's Ross and Rachel who end up married by season's enc

THE FIFTH SEASON MARKED another achievement for the show: 100 episodes.

1. The One After Ross Says Rachel

PLOT While Ross tries to undo the "I do" snafu with Emily, Monica and Chandler handle their post-coital awkwardness by agreeing to keep doin' it until they get back to New York. **INTRODUCES** The faux surname Philange (as in Dr. Philange, aka Phoebe, who's stuck in New York and is desperately trying to trick Emily's stepmom into thinking Ross has some kind of name disorder). **BEST LINE** "This is worse than when he married the lesbian." (Ross's mom) **NEW DO** Chandler **REVIEW** The screwed-up nuptials give Schwimmer a chance to be at his puppy-dog-pathetic best, while the hilariously horny adventures of Monica and Chandler—who keep getting stymied in their bid to get more London sack time—add another layer of comic franticness. **A**

2. The One With All the Kissing

PLOT Monica and Chandler continue to flout the Not in New York rule. Ross tries to woo back Emily. Rachel decides to tell Ross she's still in love with him. **BEST LINE** "I'm going to go pack my ass off." (Phoebe, who—after missing out on the London trip—wants to make the most of the group's intended outing to Atlantic City) **REVIEW** So many gems to pick from this episode: Chandler covering his absent-minded Monica smooches by repeatedly locking lips with Rachel and Phoebe; Phoebe's bitterness at all the London reminiscences; Monica's attempts to salvage Rachel's romantic life. The best scene, thanks to its sly mixture of moist-eyed melancholy and gut-busting guffaws, comes when Rachel finally tells Ross she still loves him (Ross's response: "I'm not sure what to do with that right now") and then breaks out into gales of nervous laughter. Oh yeah, and Phoebe's water breaks. **A-**

3. The One Hundredth

PLOT The gang kick off the show's 100th episode with a trip to Beth Israel Medical Center, where Phoebe gives birth to her brother's triplets. **BEST LINE** "I'm, um, Phoebe Buffay, and I have babies coming out of me." (Phoebe, upon being admitted to the hospital) **REVIEW** Although it was a nice touch to offset the "very special episode" vibe with Monica and Chandler's first fight, the whole shebang is almost completely torpedoed by a ludicrous subplot involving an Arthur Fonzarelli-obsessed obstetrician. Luckily Phoebe (who, in the Fonz plot's defense, does get to use the word "dilated-amundo") ends the episode on a high note with her sweet interaction with the newborn trio ("Little high fives"). **B**

4. The One Where Phoebe Hates PBS

PLOT Phoebe and Joey (who lands a gig on a PBS telethon) engage in the age-old "Is there such a thing as altruism?" debate (she says yes, he says no). Ross, who's still dealing with his post-nuptial fallout, gets an ultimatum from Emily: She'll move to New York to be with him if he promises never to see Rachel again. **HISTORIC MOMENT** We discover that after Phoebe's mom, Lily, died, Phoebe wrote a letter to *Sesame Street* that went unanswered—the show sent a key chain instead. **BEST LINE** "I just gave birth to three children, and I will not let them be raised in a world where Joey is right." (Phoebe) **REVIEW** Ross's tortured approach to Emily's ultimatum results in a beautifully Shakespearean denouement: An in-the-dark Rachel advises him to do whatever he has to do to make his marriage work. **B+**

5. The One With the Kips

PLOT Tired of having to sneak around, Monica and Chandler decide to go away for the weekend (with disastrous results). Ross finally tells Rachel about Emily's ultimatum. Fearing she's the new Kip (i.e., Chandler's old roommate who, after dating and breaking up with Monica was ostracized from the group), Rachel tries to get a surprisingly receptive Phoebe to start a new gang. **HISTORIC MOMENT** Joey

finds out about M&C. **BEST LINE** "So I'm thinking basically we pick it up, and then we flip it." (Joey's plan for flipping Monica's mattress) **REVIEW** A mostly plodding affair save for two priceless frames: the look on hypercritical Monica's face when Chandler admonishes her with "Jeez, relax, Mom" and the look on Joey's mug when he finally realizes his roomie is doing it with Ross's sister. **B**

6. The One With the Yeti

PLOT Emily's coming to town, which means it's time for Ross to follow through on his pledge to not see Rachel. Phoebe receives an heirloom mink coat from Phoebe Sr. Rachel starts the mating dance with the titular hairy beast, aka new neighbor Danny. **INTRODUCES** George Newbern (*Scandal*) as Danny.

1. Ross with parents Jack and Judy after his bungled nuptials. 2. Chandler kisses Rachel in a poor attempt to hide his relationship with Monica. 3. Phoebe gives birth to her half brother's triplets.

BEST LINE "Okay, let's get some perspective, people; it's not like I'm wearing a seeing-eye dog coat!" (Phoebe) **REVIEW** Phoebe's fur dilemma is mildly diverting, but the combo of Rachel and Danny doesn't exactly generate sparks. Only the sight of Schwimmer's face when he realizes he's staring down divorce No. 2 (Emily decides she can't ever fully trust him) helps revive things. **C**

7. The One Where Ross Moves In

PLOT After getting booted out of his sublet by Emily's cousin, Ross bunks with Joey and Chandler. Rachel and Danny continue their flirtation. **BEST LINE** "We...Will...We...Will...Call You Back." (The message—sung to the tune of "We Will Rock You"—that Ross immediately places on Chandler and Joey's answering machine) **REVIEW** Sure, we realize the other folks need a full day in the sun now and again, but Ross's nerdiness doesn't really satisfy the humor jones the way M&C's randy behavior has. **C**

8. The One With All the Thanksgivings

PLOT It's flashback time again, as the gang recall their worst Thanksgivings. **HISTORIC MOMENTS** Turns out Monica was motivated to lose weight after she overheard Chandler (whom she was crushing on) tell Ross: "I don't want to be stuck here all night with your fat sister." Back in real time, Chandler says "I love you" to Monica (she has a turkey carcass on her head at the time; see sidebar), but that's neither here nor there. **BEST LINE** "It's not so much an underpant as it is a feat of engineering." (Joey, singing the praises of the thong) **NEW DO** Chandler, Ross **REVIEW** In addition to all the great sight gags the episode is chock-full of juicy info: In addition to the Monica revelation, we learn that Chandler is missing the top of one of his toes thanks to an errant knife wielded by a trying-to-be-seductive (but hugely failing) Monica. **B+**

9. The One With Ross's Sandwich

PLOT Joey starts to crack under the pressure of knowing Monica and Chandler's secret. Ross experiences office rage after someone at work steals his post-Thanksgiving sandwich (complete with "the moist-maker"). **BEST LINE** "He takes naked pictures of us, and then he eats chicken, and then he looks at them." (Rachel, who thinks that Joey is the one who snapped the accidentally discovered nudie shot of Monica) **REVIEW** Exploring Ross's dark side is always a hoot, and getting a glimpse of M&C's kinkiness is an unexpected treat, but we certainly could have lived without Phoebe and Rachel's paper-thin literature class subplot. Still, two out of three ain't bad. **B+**

10. The One With the Inappropriate Sister

PLOT Ross is put on a forced sabbatical. Phoebe gets a job collecting Christmas donations. Rachel and Danny (who's the one with the out-of-line sibling) finally go out on a real date. **BEST LINE** Ross: "Hey! I am not unemployed, I am on sabbatical." Joey: "Hey, don't get all religious on me, okay!" **REVIEW** Watching Ross browbeat Joey into writing a screenplay is irksome, especially since it takes away from Joey and Chandler's far more interesting game of "fireball" (tennis ball + lighter fluid = scorching good fun). **C**

11. The One With All the Resolutions

PLOT Chandler resolves not to make fun of the gang for a whole week; Joey plans to learn guitar; Ross vows to do something he's never done before every day; Rachel swears off gossiping; Monica promises to snap more photos; Phoebe wants to fly a jet. **HISTORIC MOMENT** Rachel finds out about M&C when she overhears them planning a dirty rendezvous. **BEST LINE** "I don't know the actual names of the chords, but I made up names for the way my hands look while I'm doing them. So then this is Bear Claw, Turkey Leg and Old Lady. " (Phoebe, to Joey) **REVIEW** Who knew Chandler's forced restraint could be just as funny as his barb-zinging? Phoebe's attempt to teach Joey how to strum also amuses. But, by far, the apex comes via Ross's from-bad-to-worse interaction with lotion, baby powder and a pair of leather pants. **B+**

Let's Talk Turkey

HOW A GIANT BIRD BECAME A PIVOTAL PROP IN CHANDLER AND MONICA'S LOVE STORY.

By Amy Wilkinson

By season 5, the *Friends* Thanksgiving episode was as much a holiday tradition as cranberry sauce and pumpkin pie. So for the series' fifth such outing, producers went big—as in a giant turkey carcass.

Through flashback, we learned that Joey's worst Thanksgiving was the one in which he got Monica's basting bird stuck on his head. The gag comes full-circle, as Monica stuffs her own head into a turkey to cheer up Chandler. His reaction wasn't what she expected—after she performed a little shimmy, he blurted out: "I love you."

"We were always very concerned about [doing things] you've never seen before, and this seem[ed] like the perfect moment for the first 'I love you,'" writer Greg Malins told *EW*.

Now, if you were worried that the smell of raw poultry may have fowled up the mood, don't fret—that turkey was totally fake. "I wanted a real turkey… because I wanted Matt to have to put his head into a turkey," Malins said. "The prop department did their due diligence, but it didn't exist." So a foam model with mesh and vents for breathing was fashioned instead. (Giblets not included.)

↑ Cox rehearsed with a half-constructed turkey before filming with the finished product.

9. Joey finds a nude pic of Monica. **12.** Ross consoles himself by sleeping with Janice. **14.** Phoebe tries to "seduce" Chandler.

12. The One With Chandler's Work Laugh

PLOT Ross is taking an anger-management class. Chandler takes Monica to an office party. Rachel tries to get Monica to fess up about her relationship with Chandler. **HISTORIC MOMENT** A clearly despondent Ross hooks up with (are you sitting down?) Janice! **BEST LINE** "I guess that's two out of three… Joey." (Janice) **REVIEW** Monica's win-at-all-costs approach to a tennis game with Chandler's boss provides some major yuks, while the hookup between Ross and Janice (who eventually breaks up with him because—get this—he's too whiny) provides some major yecchs! **B+**

13. The One With Joey's Bag

PLOT Rachel dresses Joey for an audition—introducing him to the "man's bag" concept. Phoebe's grandma dies. **HISTORIC MOMENT** Phoebe finally comes face to face with her long-lost father. **CREATIVE CASTING** Bob Balaban (*Severance*) as Frank Buffay Sr. **BEST LINE** "She gives the worst massages ever! Okay, it was like she was torturing me for information." (Chandler, on Monica) **REVIEW** Phoebe's granny dying is a downer surpassed only by the lethargy of Balaban's Frank Sr. A grating appearance by Ursula and the whole annoying man's bag thing rounds off a forgettable outing. **C-**

↓ **BEST EPISODE**

14. The One Where Everybody Finds Out

PLOT The title pretty much says it all: Monica and Chandler's relationship becomes public knowledge. **HISTORIC MOMENT** We say so long to Ugly Naked Guy, who's spotted packing up his apartment, spurring homeless Ross to make a bid for his space. **BEST LINE** "They don't know that we know they know we know." (Phoebe) **REVIEW** Although the group discovery would have been riveting enough, the ensuing ron-delet of one-upmanship between Monica and Chandler and Rachel and Phoebe (who screws with Chandler's brain by trying to seduce him) is pure genius. **A**

15. The One With the Girl Who Hits Joey

PLOT Joey's getting abused by his playful punch-happy new girlfriend Katie. Ross alienates his new building mates when he refuses to ante up $100 for a handyman's retirement gift. **CREATIVE CASTING** Soleil Moon Frye as Joey's aggressive squeeze Katie and Willie Garson (*Sex and the City*) as one of Ross's neigh-bors. **BEST LINE** "Can you imagine how hard she's going to hit me when I tell her I'm taking away the Joey love?" (Joey, before break-ing up with Katie) **REVIEW** The pummeling-chick shtick would be completely yawn-inducing if it weren't for the sight of Joey wearing six sweaters for extra padding. The pariah Ross stuff, meanwhile, hits the spot as does Chandler's misguided—but nonetheless gasp-inducing—proposal gone wrong. **B**

16. The One With the Cop

PLOT Joey has a romantic dream about Monica. Phoebe goes power mad after finding a police-man's badge. **INTRODUCES** Michael

16. Phoebe starts dating a cop (Michael Rapaport). **21.** Monica and Ross get competitive about a ball game…again. **22.** Monica tackles Rachel in order to administer her eye drops. **24.** Monica and Chandler roll the dice on getting married. **24.** But it's Rachel and Ross who actually tie the knot.

Rapaport as Gary, Phoebe's man-in-blue fling. **BEST LINE** "Pivot!" (Ross) **REVIEW** In the oh-so-successful slapstick department: Ross, Chandler and Rachel trying to get Ross's new couch into his apartment. **B+**

17. The One With Rachel's Inadvertent Kiss

PLOT Rachel interviews for a job at Ralph Lauren. Joey has a flirtation with a gal who lives in Ross's apartment building. Monica and Chandler's status as steamiest couple gets threatened by the on-fire Phoebe and Gary (who even managed to violate "section 12, paragraph 7 of the criminal code"). **BEST LINE** "She lives in, like, some hot-girl parallel universe or something." (Joey, who can't locate the exact apartment his flirtee lives in) **REVIEW** Aniston bumbles through the hiring process beautifully. Ross's window shenanigans (he mimes surfing and a shark attack) provide backup guffaws, and it's all topped off by a sweet speech from Chandler convincing Monica that he's happier at this stage of their relationship than ever. Aw, shucks. **B+**

18. The One Where Rachel Smokes

PLOT Phoebe and Monica are planning a surprise early birthday party for Rachel, who takes up smoking to feel more in the loop with her puff-happy new boss. Little Ben and Joey are up for parts in the same commercial. **BEST LINE** "You've got to push past this, okay? Because it's about to get sooo good." (Ex-smoker Chandler, trying to convince Rachel to keep on lighting up) **REVIEW** The fact that an employee can feel pressured into smoking to stay connected may be a wry social observation, but it's not exactly the stuff laughs are made of. Ditto the competitive vibe between Joey and stage-dad Ross. **C**

19. The One Where Ross Can't Flirt

PLOT What little there is involves Joey inviting his Italian grandmother over to watch his stint on *Law & Order* (too bad he got edited out), Rachel and Phoebe losing one of the earrings Chandler bought Monica, and Ross flirting (horrendously) with the pizza

delivery girl. **BEST LINE** "You know that smell gas has?" (Ross's pathetic attempt at starting seductive conversation) **REVIEW** You know that smell a really bad episode has? We all could have gotten along just fine without ever meeting Joey's "Nonni" (who seems painfully corny and out of place). The episode's main highlight is getting a peek at Chandler's secretly videotaped rendition of "Space Oddity." **C-**

20. The One With the Ride-Along

PLOT Joey, Ross and Chandler do a tour of police duty in Gary's patrol car; a gunshot-sounding car backfire prompts Joey to throw his body on his sandwich (leading Chandler to think he tried to save Ross and not him). Rachel hears (and accidentally deletes) Emily's phone message for Ross, in which she posits a reconciliation. **BEST LINE** "I'd hate to have to save your life and kick your ass on the same day." (Joey, to an annoyingly grateful Ross) **REVIEW** What can you say about an episode whose most-fleshed-out plot revolves around a grown man protecting a meatball hero? Oh, we know: You can say, "Better luck next week." **C-**

21. The One With the Ball

PLOT Gary wants Phoebe to move in with him. Rachel buys a $1,000 hairless "purebred, show-quality Sphinx cat" (dubbed Mrs. Whiskerson). Joey, Ross, Monica and Chandler throw a ball back and forth for nearly 17 hours. **BEST LINE** "A minion of the Antichrist." (Chandler's description of Rachel's pet) **REVIEW** The ball-throwing thing gives us a chance to spend some good quality time with Competitive Monica, while Gary's *NYPD Blue*-esque interrogation of a reluctant-to-shack-up Phoebe tickles the rest of our ribs. **B**

22. The One With Joey's Big Break

PLOT Phoebe is mad at Ross but doesn't really remember why (it turns out to be based on a dream). And Joey, who nabbed a lead in a Vegas-based indie film, gets super-duper mad at Chandler for not believing this role will actually be the wannabe star's big break. **BEST LINE** "Let's just say there's a well-dressed pack of dogs in Ohio." (Joey, who purposely ditched Chandler's sweater vests after an aborted road trip to Vegas) **REVIEW** The bad blood between Joey and Chandler (who wants to say he's sorry with a basket of porn) adds a sweet tinge of melancholy to the usual guffaws. In fact, when the Vegas film's financing falls through and Joey plummets from leading man to Trojan-costumed casino underling, the big lug's plight really pulls at your heartstrings. **B**

23. The One in Vegas, Part 1

PLOT To celebrate their first anniversary, Monica buys Chandler tickets to visit Joey in Vegas (the gang tag along). Chandler discovers that Monica had lunch with Richard. **BEST LINE** "Love your condoms, my man." (Chandler, to Joey, who's still working the Trojan gig) **REVIEW** Rachel and Ross hold up their end of the episode by trying to out-embarrass each other on their flight to Sin City. But, alas, Phoebe (who's still smarting from being left behind on the London jaunt) and Joey (who's found—God help us!—his "identical hand twin") have had better days. **B**

24. The One In Vegas, Part 2

PLOT The mustache and beard that Ross drew on Rachel's face during the last episode's coda won't come off. Joey still has dreams of making hand-twin millions. Monica and Chandler make up. Slot-playing Phoebe has a set-to with a "lurker" (an old woman who tries to score on the machines Phoebe leaves behind). **HISTORIC MOMENT** Ross and Rachel get married. **BEST LINE** "I am a human doodle." (Rachel, bemoaning her ink-stained mug) **REVIEW** Not even Joey's continued hand-twin craziness can mar this most excellent episode. The jaw-dropping surprise of watching Monica and Chandler throw caution (and a hard eight) to the wind and decide to get married that very evening would have been plenty, but when a wasted Ross and Rachel exit the chapel instead—well, don't even get us started. **A-** EW

FRIENDS OF *FRIENDS*

Best Celebrity Guest Stars

Forget the Ivy—Stage 24 on the Warner Bros. Studios lot was Hollywood's hottest hangout in the '90s and early '00s. *By Marc Snetiker and Amy Wilkinson*

George Clooney and Noah Wyle

"The One With Two Parts"

(SEASON 1)

The *ER* hunks appeared as—this is a stretch—cute doctors (incidentally, ones *not* named Ross and Carter) who went out with Monica and Rachel.

Tom Selleck

(SEASONS 2, 3 AND 6)

Magnum P.I. himself romanced Monica as Dr. Richard Burke, a friend of Monica's father and Chandler's biggest competition. (Also of note: A pre-*Alias* Michael Vartan played his son Timothy… whom Monica also had the hots for, briefly. Those Burkes!)

Julia Roberts

"The One After the Super Bowl: Part 2" (SEASON 2)

America's Sweetheart got sweet revenge as Susie, who stole Chandler's clothes, stranding him in the restroom. Matthew Perry later revealed in his 2022 memoir *Friends, Lovers and the Big Terrible Thing* that he had to write Roberts a paper on quantum physics to persuade her to take on the cameo.

Isabella Rossellini

"The One With Frank Junior"

(SEASON 3)

Poor Ross. After he swaps in local Winona Ryder for international Isabella Rossellini on his list of five famous people he's allowed to sleep with, who should walk into Central Perk but the beautiful *Blue Velvet* actress. She was all poise when Ross embarrassingly admitted that she was an "alternate."

Billy Crystal and Robin Williams

"The One With the Ultimate Fighting Champion"

(SEASON 3)

The two funnymen caused quite the stir at the coffeehouse when they sat next to the gang and proceeded to have a very loud, very personal conversation. (Crystal's Tim was cheating with the wife of Williams's Tomas.) If you've watched the oddball scene recently, you probably won't be surprised to learn it was completely improvised by the actors.

Reese Witherspoon

(SEASON 6)

The actress, who appeared in two episodes, was utterly perfect as Rachel's even-more-spoiled little sister Jill, who shook up her sib when she briefly dated Ross.

↓ Classmates Susie and Chandler reunite.

↑ Clockwise from left Will with fellow "I Hate Rachel Green" club member Ross; Eric and Phoebe attempt dating, but it's weird; Rachel tries to deal with her sister Amy.

Bruce Willis
(SEASON 6)

The action star was in three episodes and won an Emmy—and got to hook up with Jennifer Aniston—playing the intimidating father of Ross's student girlfriend.

Susan Sarandon
"The One With Joey's New Brain" (SEASON 7)

Sarandon played a soap diva (think Susan Lucci) who struck up a romance with Joey after he let it slip that her character would be killed.

Winona Ryder
"The One With Rachel's Big Kiss" (SEASON 7)

Nobody believed that Rachel had actually kissed her former sorority sister, played with hilarious closeted enthusiasm by Ryder.

Sean Penn
(SEASON 8)

The Oscar winner appeared on two episodes as Ursula's boyfriend Eric. Famously "anti-Hollywood," Penn was persuaded to guest-star by his two kids, who were fans of the show.

Brad Pitt
"The One With the Rumor" (SEASON 8)

Aniston's then husband starred in a Thanksgiving episode, playing a very different role: as Will, a founding member of the "I Hate Rachel Green" club.

Alec Baldwin
(SEASON 8)

A pre-*30 Rock* Baldwin appeared as Phoebe's overly enthusiastic date Parker. ("I wanna take a mental picture of you all!")

Paul Rudd
(SEASONS 9 AND 10)

Phoebe's best chance at normalcy was marrying geeky pianophile Mike, who became a beloved member of the group during 17 episodes.

Christina Applegate
(SEASONS 9 AND 10)

Rachel's other sister was the despicably witless Amy, who didn't know her niece's name yet still wanted custody if her parents died. Criminally, Applegate's only Emmy win to this day is for this role.

Jeff Goldblum
"The One With the Mugging" (SEASON 9)

Joey wants to impress legendary director Leonard Hayes (Goldblum) with his audition, and miraculously, a full bladder helps him do it. EW

SEASON 6

Ross and Monica try to make the cut on *Dick Clark's New Year's Rockin' Eve*.

Making Moves

New relationships, new jobs and New Year's Eve dances—everyone's life seems in flux this season. You could say it's anything but routine

SEASON 6 FOUND A TRIO OF high-profile guest-stars (Elle Macpherson, Bruce Willis and the returning Tom Selleck) complicating the Friends' love lives. Willis earned an Emmy for playing Paul Stevens (a role that came to be after losing a bet with Matthew Perry).

4

1. The One After Vegas

PLOT Ross and Rachel wake up hungover—and with no memory of having been married. Chandler and Monica decide to live together. **INTRODUCES** The newly married Courteney Cox Arquette (the rest of the cast append Arquette to their names in the opening credits in a show of solidarity). **HISTORIC MOMENT** It's implied that Phoebe was previously married in Vegas and never got a divorce (she thought it meant that you were married only in Vegas). **BEST LINE** "This is not a marriage—this is the world's worst hangover!" (Rachel, to Ross) **REVIEW** The episode's biggest yuks come courtesy of Schwimmer and Aniston, who spin new variations on Ross's and Rachel's twisted romantic fates. **B+**

2. The One Where Ross Hugs Rachel

PLOT Chandler and Monica break the news to Joey and Rachel that they're moving in together, and Phoebe urges Ross to tell Rachel that he hasn't annulled their Vegas nuptials. **BEST LINE** "We were drunk—I would've married Joey with that amount of alcohol." (Ross, about his marriage to Rachel) **REVIEW** Joey's emotional reaction to Chandler moving out is both funny and touching—we know how much these guys love being roommates. But Rachel's emotionless reaction is a little hard to buy: Why would she think Chandler and Monica aren't really going to shack up? **B**

3. The One With Ross's Denial

PLOT Rachel proposes moving in with Phoebe, but the latter says she has a roommate named Denise. Ross suggests Rachel move in with him, and she accepts—not knowing they're still married. **BEST LINE** "You love her again—you relove her!" (Phoebe, to Ross, re: Rachel) **REVIEW** It's fun to see Monica and Chandler fight after their lovey-dovey behavior (he wants to put arcade games and his Barcalounger in Monica's tastefully decorated apartment). Joey's search for a "nonsmoking, non-ugly" female roommate also scores, but it's Ross's increasingly desperate attempts to deceive Rachel that make this episode so amusing. **A-**

4. The One Where Joey Loses His Insurance

PLOT Rachel takes a message from Ross's divorce lawyer and finds out he hasn't annulled their marriage. Joey's SAG health insurance expires. A psychic tells Phoebe she's going to die within a week, but the fortune teller expires instead. **BEST LINE** "That's weird. I don't remember being in a movie called *Benefits Lapsed*." (Joey thinking he's received a residuals check) **REVIEW** This hit-and-miss installment mostly misses. The health-insurance subplot is both predictable and

4. Rachel and Monica get into a quarrel over candlesticks. **7.** Joey gets a new roommate (played by supermodel Elle Macpherson). **8.** Ross goes a little overboard on the teeth whitening. **9.** Rachel's Thanksgiving trifle does not go to plan.

icky (Joey develops a hernia as soon as his coverage runs out), and Monica and Rachel's squabble over a pair of candlesticks is a time waster. **B-**

5. The One With Joey's Porsche

PLOT Joey finds the keys to a Porsche at Central Perk and pretends that it's his to attract chicks. Rachel and Ross finally apply for an annulment. **HISTORIC MOMENTS** Phoebe asks Rachel to be her roommate (the still-unseen Denise is out of town until Dec. 26); Rachel admits it was her idea to marry Ross in Vegas. **BEST LINE** "When—after the birth of our first secret child?" (Rachel, asking Ross when he was going to tell her they were still married) **REVIEW** Even though it's a blatant product placement, the Porsche gives the increasingly confident LeBlanc a chance to strut his comic stuff. **B**

6. The One on the Last Night

PLOT On the eve of M&C moving in together, Rachel isn't packed, so Monica organizes the gang to get the job done. Joey declines Chandler's offer to lend him money to get by until he finds a new roomie, so he has to come up with ways to give him cash by creating a fake game called Cups. **BEST LINE** "Hurry! Monica's going to make you pack! She's got jobs for everyone! Now it's too late for me, but save yourselves!" (Phoebe, to the guys) **REVIEW** Schwimmer shows a sure hand directing the ensemble in this episode. Monica and Rachel's catfight is uproarious, as are Chandler's schemes to supplement Joey's income. Plus Monica and Chandler's farewells to their roomies are genuinely affecting. **A-**

7. The One Where Phoebe Runs

PLOT Joey introduces the gang to his new roommate, leggy Australian dancer Janine Lecroix. Phoebe's loose-limbed jogging style embarrasses Rachel. **INTRODUCES** Supermodel Elle Macpherson as Janine. **BEST LINE** "When she runs, she looks like a cross between Kermit the Frog and the Six Million Dollar Man." (Rachel on Phoebe) **REVIEW** Macpherson is naturally funny, and LeBlanc's panicky reactions to her are downright hysterical. **B**

8. The One With Ross's Teeth

PLOT Phoebe asks Rachel if she can use the copy machine at her office. Pheebs says she made out with Ralph Lauren (though she's actually hooked up with a copy boy). **CREATIVE CASTING** Ralph Lauren as himself. **BEST LINE** "Oh, are you setting Ross up with someone? Does she have a wedding dress?" (Rachel to Monica) **REVIEW** The repeated references to Ralph Lauren as "the silver fox" feel like a forced attempt to suck up to him so they can use his name on the show. Schwimmer does what he can with the one-joke subplot about Ross's overly bleached teeth, but the episode ultimately lacks bite. **C-**

9. The One Where Ross Got High

PLOT Monica's parents, who have never liked Chandler, are coming to Thanksgiving dinner, and he's determined to win them over.

13. Ross briefly dates Rachel's sister Jill (Reese Witherspoon). **15.** Rachel imagines what her life would have been like had she married Barry. **17.** Rachel and Phoebe practice their self-defense skills on Ross.

Phoebe confesses she had a romantic dream about Mr. Geller, and Janine invites Ross and Joey to join her dancer friends' feast. **BEST LINE** "Whoa—snowin' out there?" (Chandler, accidentally calling attention to Mr. Geller's dandruff) **REVIEW** There are many reasons to give thanks for this episode: the always-welcome return of Elliott Gould and Christina Pickles as Monica and Ross's folks; Perry's masterful hemming and hawing as he digs himself deeper and deeper with them; and Rachel's deliciously awful cooking (she mistakenly combines the recipes for English trifle and shepherd's pie). It's a comedic cornucopia! **A-**

10. The One With the Routine

PLOT Janine lands a job dancing at a pre-taping of *Dick Clark's New Year's Rockin' Eve* and asks Joey, Ross and Monica to join her (the Gellers' dorky dream come true). Phoebe and Rachel recruit Chandler in their annual search for the presents Monica bought for them. **BEST LINE** "Ross, I think we should stick to the routine. We don't want to look stupid." (Monica) **REVIEW** The Dick Clark plotline rocks—it brings out Monica's and Ross's inner geeks, and the retro "routine" Cox and Schwimmer perform in an attempt to get onto one of the platforms is sheer genius. But the stuff about the hidden gifts seems kinda juvenile—aren't these characters, like, in their 30s now? **B**

11. The One With the Apothecary Table

PLOT Rachel orders an apothecary table from Pottery Barn, unaware that Phoebe hates all mass-produced furniture. Joey and Janine are now officially an item. One problem: She dislikes Monica and Chandler. **BEST LINE** "Ah, just like the apothecary tables of yore." (Chandler, after Rachel said her table holds 300 CDs) **REVIEW** The twist of Janine not caring for Chandler ("blah") and Monica ("very loud for such a small person") is inspired. So is the mockery of the omnipresent Pottery Barn, which almost makes its mailbox-clogging catalogs seem worthwhile. **B+**

12. The One With the Joke

PLOT A joke Ross says he wrote gets printed by *Playboy*—but Chandler claims credit for it. Joey gets a job as a waiter at Central Perk. **BEST LINE** "I was an actor, and now I'm a waiter. You're supposed to go in the other direction." (Joey) **REVIEW** With the Janine arc completed and Chandler and Monica happily cohabiting, not a whole lot happens in this palatable but instantly forgettable episode. **C**

13. The One With Rachel's Sister

PLOT Rachel gets a surprise visit from her spoiled younger sister Jill, who ends up going out on a date with Ross. Monica comes down with a cold, and Chandler's grossed out by her phlegmy come-ons. **INTRODUCES** Reese Witherspoon as Jill. **BEST LINE** "I don't like it when Ross goes out with anyone but with my sister? Isn't that, like, incest?" (Rachel) **REVIEW** Witherspoon's a riot as Rachel's even-more-princessy sister. If only Cox's fake stuffy-nose act were as believable—although it is pretty funny when Chandler finally gets turned on by watching Monica rub Vicks on her chest. **B+**

14. The One Where Chandler Can't Cry

PLOT Rachel's beside herself over her sister dating Ross, which only makes Jill more attracted to him. Strangers start recognizing Phoebe Buffay from porno movies—which actually star her sister, who's been using Phoebe's name. **BEST LINE** "Yes, it was very sad when the guy stopped drawing the deer." (Chandler, explaining why he didn't cry when Bambi's mother died) **REVIEW** Witherspoon and Aniston continue to work together beautifully—too bad Reese didn't stick around after this episode. The porno subplot will make you scream (among Phoebe's alleged titles: *Lawrence of a Labia* and *Buffay the Vampire Layer*), and Chandler's attempts to turn on, and eventually off, the waterworks will make you cry—with laughter. **A-**

15-16. The One That Could Have Been, Parts 1 & 2

PLOT Rachel announces that her ex-fiancé Barry and best friend, Mindy, are getting a divorce, and she wonders what life would be like if she had gotten married to him. The gang also imagine a parallel universe in which Ross never divorced Carol, Chandler pursued a writing career, Monica was still fat, Phoebe was a stockbroker, and Joey remained as Dr. Drake Ramoray on *Days of Our Lives*. **INTRODUCES** Cole Sprouse as Ben. **CREATIVE CASTING** Kristian Alfonso as Hope Brady (her *Days of Our Lives* character) and Paul Gleason (*The Breakfast Club*) as Phoebe's boss. **NEW DO** Phoebe, Monica, Rachel **BEST LINE** "Well, with Dr. Drake, they always tell me what to say, and with Joey, I pretty much have to make it up on my own." (Joey) **REVIEW** Yes, it's the last refuge of sitcom writers who've run out of new ideas: the "what-if" episode. Which raises the question, What if you never wasted an hour of your life watching this forced groaner? **D+**

17. The One With "Unagi"

PLOT Phoebe and Rachel start taking a self-defense class, and ex-karate student Ross teaches them about "unagi"—a state of total awareness that prepares you for any danger. Chandler and Monica don't know what to make each other for their belated Valentine's Day presents. Joey's hard up for cash, so he signs up for a medical experiment on identical twins and hires another actor, Carl, to pose as his brother. **CREATIVE CASTING** Louis Mandylor (*My Big Fat Greek Wedding*) as Carl. **BEST LINE** "Hey, remember

↓ Co-creators David Crane and Marta Kauffman with David Schwimmer on the *Friends* set in 1999.

The One With the Episode Titles

SERIES CO-CREATOR DAVID CRANE EXPLAINS THE SHOW S UNIQUE APPROACH TO NAMING ITS INSTALLMENTS. ***By Samantha Highfill***

Episode naming conventions (be it *Grey's Anatomy*'s song titles or *The Big Bang Theory*'s faux science terminology) are commonplace now, but when *Friends* debuted in 1994, the idea was new. *Friends'* approach was straightforward: Each started with "The One" and went from there. There was "The One With the Football," "The One Where No One's Ready," "The One Where Everybody Finds Out" (you get the idea). And for co-creators David Crane and Marta Kauffman, that simplicity came from experience. "We'd been on shows where everyone's trying to come up with really pun-y titles, and that is not the best use of anyone's time. Let's cut to the chase; it's the one with the thing, and now we can move on to actually working on the show itself," Crane said. "Because that's how you always refer to a TV show: 'Did you see the one with the thing?'"

19. Ross tries to hang with his much younger girlfriend Elizabeth (Alexandra Holden). **20.** Joey auditions for the lead role opposite a robot in *Mac and C.H.E.E.S.E.* **21.** Ross meets his girlfriend's father (played by Bruce Willis). **24.** Richard (Tom Selleck) makes a final return to woo Monica.

when I had a monkey? What was I thinking?" (Ross) **REVIEW** The word "unagi" sounds more and more absurd every time Schwimmer says it, but it's Joey's attempts to train Carl to behave exactly like him that make this another standout episode for this season's MVP, LeBlanc. **B+**

18. The One Where Ross Dates a Student

PLOT One of Ross's students, Elizabeth, calls him "the hottie of the paleontology department" in her evaluation, and he accepts her offer for a date. Joey gets an audition for a new Al Pacino movie. A fire damages Phoebe and Rachel's place, so Phoebe moves into Monica's pad, and Rachel shacks up with Joey. **INTRODUCES** Alexandra Holden as Elizabeth. **BEST LINE** "It actually is in the handbook. I can't date you or have a hot plate in my office." (Ross, to Elizabeth) **REVIEW** Ross's relationship with Elizabeth is simultaneously one of the most boring and creepiest romances in *Friends'* history. The apartment-fire story line comes out of the blue, but pairing up Joey and Rachel in the same apartment will pay big comedic dividends in future episodes. One question: Why no mention that Joey was once Pacino's butt double? **B-**

19. The One With Joey's Fridge

PLOT Joey's broke and can't afford to fix the fridge, so he eats everything before it goes bad. Chandler and Monica compete with Phoebe to find Rachel the right guy. Ross introduces the gang to Elizabeth, but he gets jealous when she leaves for spring break in Daytona without him. **BEST LINE** "So, I will take one box of the Thin Mints." (Ross, covering when another professor walks in on him and Elizabeth) **REVIEW** Whenever a major plotline revolves around one of the characters' appliances, you know the writers are getting low on material. **C+**

20. The One With Mac and C.H.E.E.S.E.

PLOT Joey wins an audition for a leading role in a sci-fi television show, playing detective "Mac" Machiavelli opposite a Computerized Humanoid Electronically Enhanced Secret Enforcer, or "C.H.E.E.S.E." But Chandler's poor message-taking means he misses the final callback. **BEST LINE** "If I don't get this part, I'm never gonna eat macaroni and cheese again! No, I didn't say that! That doesn't count." (Joey) **NEW DO** Everyone **REVIEW** Don't be fooled: This is a clip show, and a pretty

24

random one at that. The montages include...the Friends' various travails at work, Chandler and Joey's hugs over the years and the characters' many fights. While Joey ultimately gets the role, you can't get around the fact that this is essentially a glorified rerun. **D+**

21. The One Where Ross Meets Elizabeth's Dad

PLOT Ross is worried about meeting his girlfriend's disapproving father, who ends up making out with Rachel. Meanwhile, Joey's nervous about his big *Mac and C.H.E.E.S.E.* gig, especially after agent Estelle tells him that he's about to be fired. **INTRODUCES** Bruce Willis (Perry's costar in *The Whole Nine Yards*) as Paul Stevens, Elizabeth's dad. **BEST LINE** "The lead in my own TV series? I've dreamed about this for years! Why have I not been preparing?" (Joey) **REVIEW** The female Friends' drooling over Willis (who won an Emmy for this stint) is distastefully reminiscent of their hard-to-swallow reaction to Jean-Claude Van Damme in the Super Bowl episode. Thank God for LeBlanc, who milks the *Mac and C.H.E.E.S.E.* gags for all they're worth. **C+**

22. The One Where Paul's the Man

PLOT Ross and Elizabeth take a trip to her family's cabin, unaware that Paul is planning a romantic getaway with Rachel. Chandler seems to freak when he finds out Monica has put their names on a waiting list to get married at a museum. Chuffed about his TV gig, Joey battles to get his picture back on the "wall of fame" at the local dry cleaner. **BEST LINE** "Looks like I'm not the only one interested in fossils." (Ross, teasing Rachel about dating Paul) **REVIEW** The show's lame attempt to stage a door-slamming farce only proves *Frasier* did it better. **C-**

23. The One With the Ring

PLOT While Chandler searches for the perfect engagement ring for Monica, Rachel tries to get the strong, silent Paul to share his feelings. **BEST LINE** "Come on, Ross, you're a paleontologist; dig a little deeper." (Phoebe) **NEW DO** Chandler **REVIEW** Poor Willis is forced to weep uncontrollably for "comic" effect (a rerun of Perry's gag from episode 14). Luckily more emphasis is placed on Chandler's plans to pop the question. **B**

↓ **BEST EPISODES**

24-25. The One With the Proposal, Parts 1 & 2

PLOT Chandler's proposal dinner with Monica is marred by the surprise appearance of Richard, who later confesses he still loves her. Ross tires of Elizabeth's juvenile behavior and calls off the relationship. Rachel invites Joey to join her at a charity auction, where he accidentally buys a $20,000 sailboat. **HISTORIC MOMENTS** Monica gets not one, but two proposals—from Chandler and Richard. How much more historic can you get? **BEST LINE** "If you're not careful, you may not get married at all this year." (Chandler, to the oft-wed Ross) **REVIEW** Although the Richard wrinkle is a blatant deus ex machina, the romantic predicament allows Cox and Perry to deliver their finest, funniest performances to date. If you can watch the proposal scene with dry eyes, you're made of stronger stuff than we are. Plus the sight of LeBlanc in a captain's uniform alone is worth tuning in to see. **A** EW

SEASON 7

Making It Official

A season-long march to the altar—complete with runaway groom!—culminates in a beautiful wedding ceremony. And surprise pregnancy test results...

Monica and Chandler tie the knot with the help of bridesmaid Phoebe and maid of honor Rachel.

SEVEN SEASONS IN, THE SHOW WAS BEGINNING TO SHOW A FEW SIGNS OF wear. Still, the writers managed to expertly suffuse it with fun surprises, including a jaw-dropping pregnancy cliff-hanger.

↓ BEST EPISODE

1. The One With Monica's Thunder

PLOT Phoebe campaigns to provide the music at M&C's wedding; Rachel steals Monica's engagement thunder by kissing Ross; Chandler experiences erectile difficulties. **BEST LINE** "I'm sorry. Apparently I've opened the door to the past." (Monica, catching Ross and Rachel kissing outside her apartment) **REVIEW** There's nothing like a little inter-Friends psychological intrigue, and Monica's analysis that Rachel can't stand the fact that her formerly fat friend is getting married first adds some heft to the top-of-their-game comic goings-on. And the wacky Joey subplot—he's auditioning to play a 19-year-old—provides both a sidesplitting sight gag (Joey in full teen gear) and this memorable take on teen-speak: "'Sup with the wack PlayStation 'sup." **A**

2. The One With Rachel's Book

PLOT Monica finds out that her parents spent her wedding fund. Phoebe moves in with Ross to give M&C some space. Joey finds Rachel's dirty novel. **BEST LINE** "As the groom, all you have to do is show up and try to say the right name." (Ross, imparting wedding advice to Chandler) **REVIEW** Aside from Ross getting tricked into giving a massage to an old guy and Joey's goading of erotica-loving Rachel, there's little to amuse. But you do get to see Chandler give another one of his best-boyfriend-in-the-world speeches to reassure nuptials-crazed Monica. **B-**

3. The One With Phoebe's Cookies

PLOT Monica wants Phoebe's grandmother's cookie recipe. Rachel offers to teach Joey how to sail. Monica's dad invites Chandler for a game of racquetball. **BEST LINE** "I'm my father. Oh my God. This is horrible. I've been trying so hard not to be my mother, I did not see this coming." (Rachel) **REVIEW** Rachel and Joey's blue-screened sailboat outing is a jarring flight of fancy that generates more *huh?* than *ha*. Monica and Phoebe trying to re-create the perfect chocolate chip cookie is more appealing ("Nestlé Toulouse"!), but overall this episode is not exactly the tastiest treat. **C**

4. The One With Rachel's Assistant

PLOT Rachel gets a promotion. *Mac and C.H.E.E.S.E.* debuts (and is canceled), but *Days of Our Lives* wants Joey to audition to play Drake Ramoray's twin brother, Stryker. **INTRODUCES** Eddie Cahill (*CSI: NY*) as Rachel's new assistant, Tag Jones. **BEST LINE** "Ross used to stay home every Saturday night to watch *Golden Girls*!" (Monica, revealing Ross's deep dark secrets) **REVIEW** It's another Friend vs. Friend extravaganza, as Chandler, Ross and Monica end up dishing one another's secrets (e.g., Chandler won a Vanilla Ice lookalike contest; Monica couldn't tell time until she was 13). What more could you ask for? Well, perhaps more laughs on the Joey front. **A-**

5. The One With the Engagement Picture

PLOT Monica and Chandler have

their engagement photos taken. Cute Coffeehouse Guy (Kyle, aka "Hums While He Pees") asks Phoebe out. Ross dates Hums While He Pees' ex-wife (aka Whitney). **BEST LINE** "Oooh, I could just spread him on a cracker." (Rachel, salivating over Tag) **REVIEW** Packed with rollicking Rachel high jinks, funny faces from Chandler (whose bad-photo poses are priceless) and gut-busting histrionics from caught-between-divorces Phoebe and Ross. Plus, Tag does a great Joey impression: "How *you* doin'?" **A-**

6. The One With the Nap Partners

PLOT Monica needs a maid of honor; Chandler's disgruntled ex pops up; Ross and Joey enjoy napping together. **BEST LINE** "Well,

we watch it a second time, and it's *Die Hard 2*." (Joey, on *Die Hard*) **REVIEW** Mercifully, the lame "nap partners" story line is given short shrift, allowing more screen time for Phoebe and Rachel to duke it out for M-of-H status (Rachel ultimately gets the nod). The potentially dull plot involving Chandler's ex turns into a surprisingly moving examination of Monica's weight issues and whether Chandler would still love her if she got fat again. **B**

1. Joey tries to pass as a 19-year-old for an audition. **6.** Joey and Ross discover their nap compatibility. **7.** Monica is forced to deal with a dissatisfied customer… Janice. **9.** Ross attempts to teach Phoebe how to ride a bike.

7. The One With Ross's Library Book

PLOT Joey hooks up with a gal Rachel and Phoebe come to adore. Ross finds his doctoral dissertation in the library—in the aisle where people go to have sex. Janice returns! **CREATIVE CASTING** *Sex and the City*'s Kristin Davis as Erin, Joey's intimacy-issue-afflicted new girlfriend. **BEST LINE** "Man, do you know what guys want." (Joey's sarcastic response to Phoebe when she points out that Erin speaks four languages) **NEW DO** Rachel **REVIEW** Were they trying to make the most annoying episode ever? Not only does Davis seem wildly out of place, but we have to endure a too-absurd-for-words Ross subplot and too much of Janice's whining. Uncle! **C-**

8. The One Where Chandler Doesn't Like Dogs

PLOT It's Thanksgiving, and Chandler's got the gang playing a name-all-the-states-in-six-minutes game. Phoebe's secretly dog-sitting Clunkers. Rachel tells Tag she has a crush on him. **BEST LINE** "Yeah, it's like a cow's opinion. You know, it just doesn't matter. It's 'moo.'" (Joey, misusing the term "moot point") **REVIEW** Although Ross's inability to ace the states challenge (Delaware provides a huge stumbling block) leads to some amusingly Geller-esque mania, the dog brouhaha (Chandler's afraid and "allergic") is for the birds. Still, Joey's malapropism is unforgettable. **B**

9. The One With All the Candy

PLOT Monica makes holiday candy for the neighbors. Ross buys Phoebe her first bike. Rachel's pornographic workplace evaluation of Tag "Sweet Cheeks" Jones accidentally gets sent to Human Resources. **BEST LINE** "No, no. One daddy, two mommies." (Ross, after Ben calls Chandler "Daddy")

Before They Were Stars

KEEP AN EYE OUT FOR THESE FAMOUS FACES IN EARLY ROLES.
By Marc Snetiker

Mae Whitman
"THE ONE WHERE RACHEL QUITS" (SEASON 3)
The future *Parenthood* star played Sarah Tuttle, a young Scout whom Ross accidentally knocks down a flight of stairs. Ouch!

Hugh Laurie
"THE ONE WITH ROSS' WEDDING: PT. 2" (SEASON 4)
Is there a doctor on board? A future one, yes. A pre-*House* Laurie gave a memorable turn as an annoyed passenger sitting next to Rachel on the plane to London.

Ellen Pompeo
"THE ONE WHERE THE STRIPPER CRIES" (SEASON 10)
Before scrubbing in at Seattle Grace Hospital, Pompeo guest-starred as Missy, an off-limits conquest who came between Ross and Chandler in college.

Craig Robinson
"THE ONE WITH PRINCESS CONSUELA" (SEASON 10)
Talk about gaining office experience: Robinson cameoed as a city clerk who gave Phoebe free rein to legally change her name (Princess Consuela Banana Hammock!).

Dakota Fanning
"THE ONE WITH PRINCESS CONSUELA" (SEASON 10)
It's a twofer! Joining Robinson in this episode was Dakota Fanning, playing Mackenzie, a little girl who bonded with Joey when Monica and Chandler bought the house she lived in.

Jim Rash
"THE LAST ONE: PART 2" (SEASON 10)
How does Rachel keep scoring flashy seatmates? A pre-*Community* Rash plays "Nervous Male Passenger" (yep, that's what the credit reads) on Rachel's aborted flight to Paris.

REVIEW Although the Rachel and Tag story line continues to entertain, the candy subplot leaves a bad taste in our mouths. **C**

10. The One With the Holiday Armadillo

PLOT It's Chandler and Monica's first Christmas as a betrothed couple. Ross gets Ben for the holiday. Phoebe, preparing to move back into her old apartment, hatches a plan (involving drums and a tarantula) to get Rachel to ditch Joey and become her roomie again. **BEST LINE** "My favorite part is when Superman flew all the Jews out of Egypt." (Chandler, about Ross's Joey-assisted explanation of Hanukkah) **REVIEW** Something about the holidays makes the Friends go loopy: Sure, there are chuckles to be had watching Ross dress up—for Ben's benefit—as the title's armadillo (the Santa suits were taken), but the rest of the episode is positively Grinch-like with the yuks. **B-**

11. The One With All the Cheesecakes

PLOT After Chandler steals a neighbor's cheesecake, he and Rachel become obsessed with the confection. Monica's peeved she wasn't invited to her cousin's wedding. Phoebe's ex-boyfriend David (a scientist who moved to Russia) returns. **CREATIVE CASTING** Hank Azaria returns as David, last seen in season 1, episode 10. **BEST LINE** "Oh right, like they're gonna let *me* have a passport." (Phoebe, on traveling internationally) **REVIEW** Not exactly packed with laughs (although an incensed Monica is always a joy to behold). This baby's main highlight is watching softhearted Joey try to console Phoebe, who's beside herself because the only guy she's "ever been crazy about" is heading back to Minsk. **C**

10. Dueling holiday mascots: Santa and the Holiday Armadillo. **14.** Tag (Eddie Cahill) helps Rachel celebrate her 30th birthday. **15.** Susan Sarandon guest-stars as a high-maintenance soap opera actress opposite Joey.

12. The One Where They're Up All Night

PLOT Sleeplessness all around as Ross and Joey get stuck on the roof, Chandler and Monica suffer bouts of insomnia, Phoebe battles a fire alarm, and Rachel and Tag search for some missing contracts she claims she put on his desk. **BEST LINE** "I'd prefer not to answer that right now. I'm still carrying a little holiday weight." (Ross, when Joey—whom he's using as a human ladder—asks him his weight) **REVIEW** If not for Ross and Joey's slapstick on a fire escape (and a cute scene between Rachel and slyer-than-he-looks Tag), this episode would be a snooze. And that annoying fire alarm sound? We'd take a half hour of Janice's laugh over that. **C**

13. The One Where Rosita Dies

PLOT The dead woman in question is actually Joey's Barcalounger (which Rachel accidentally destroys). Ross and Monica's parents are selling their home. Phoebe gets a telemarketing job. **HISTORIC MOMENT** The first of four supersize episodes, which ran 40 minutes to combat CBS's *Survivor*. **CREATIVE CASTING** Jason Alexander as Earl, the office manager, whom Phoebe cold-calls. **BEST LINE** "Chandler?" (Phoebe, when Earl says, "I've been working for 10 years now at this meaningless dead-end job, and nobody here even knows that I exist") **REVIEW** Not much to hang your humor hat on here, unless you think Monica's moldy childhood tchotchkes (or her newly inherited Porsche) are funny. And what's with the plug for La-Z-Boy's (fictional) E-cliner 3000 (which Chandler tells us "*Sit* magazine called chair of the year")? **C**

14. The One Where They All Turn 30

PLOT Rachel's 30th birthday gives the gang a chance to flash back to how they all dealt with the milestone—Ross bought a sports car, Phoebe rode a mile on a Hippity-Hop; Joey cursed God; that sort of thing. Oh yeah, and Rachel breaks up with Tag. **BEST LINE** "And girls, this thing is a godsend, if you know what I mean." (Phoebe, straddling the Hippity-Hop) **REVIEW** Rachel being bummed about being hubby- and childless is predictable, but the part where Phoebe learns she's really a year older than she thought is a hoot. Ditto Monica's drunken turn at her black-tie birthday party. But the apex comes when Ross enlists the gang to free his new wheels from between two parked cars. **B+**

15. The One With Joey's New Brain

PLOT Joey's character is coming out of his coma on *Days of Our Lives*. In honor of Chandler's half-Scottish heritage, Ross plans to play the bagpipes at M&C's wedding. Phoebe and Rachel vie for a date with a guy who left his cell phone at Central Perk. **CREATIVE CASTING** Susan Sarandon as soon-to-be-fired soap diva Cecilia Monroe (whose brain Joey's character is inheriting). **BEST LINE** "She is so good at throwing drinks in people's faces. I mean, I don't think I've ever seen her finish a beverage." (Rachel, about Monroe) **REVIEW** Monroe and Joey's romantic fling

20. Ross gets a little too cozy with his cousin (Denise Richards). **23.** Rachel purloins Monica's Porsche. **24.** Phoebe finds a positive pregnancy test in Monica's bathroom and assumes it's hers. **25.** Monica and Chandler finally make it down the aisle.

helps block the pain of Ross's bagpiping, and bless the writer who came up with the gag about Joey confusing Guadalajara with LaGuardia (Airport). **B**

16. The Stuff You've Never Seen

PLOT Conan O'Brien hosts what is essentially a *Friends* blooper special that also milks seven years of nostalgia. **REVIEW** The Mona Lisa of flashback episodes. Along with highlighting the cast's unparalleled chemistry and the writers' strokes of genius, this pretty much supplies a half hour's worth of raison d'être for the episode guide you currently hold. **A**

17. The One With the Truth About London

PLOT Ross asks Rachel to watch Ben. M&C are searching for an officiant. Joey decides to be ordained over the Internet. **BEST LINE** "Internet ministers can still have sex, right?" (Joey) **REVIEW** Rachel teaches Ben a bunch of practical jokes to play on Dad, but the episode's best parts revolve around M&C's fateful night in London, including the revelation that Monica was originally looking for a meaningless hookup with Joey. Mr. Tribbiani definitely wins the episode's MVP award for his surprisingly poignant tribute to M&C's relationship. **B+**

18. The One With the Cheap Wedding Dress

PLOT A gown war between Monica and a fellow bride-to-be results in her having to choose between her favorite dress and Chandler's favorite wedding band. Joey and Ross date the same girl. **CREATIVE CASTING** Gabrielle Union as *Friends*' first Black love interest. **BEST LINE** "I have an oily T-zone." (Ross, to Joey, who makes fun of him for having face cream) **REVIEW** The Good: We get a short but sweet taste of type A Monica (before she gives up the gown). The Bad: yet another Friends-vying-for-the-same-date plot? The (delightfully) Ugly: Joey and Ross dish on each other in front of the girl (e.g., Joey tells her Ross slept in the same bed as a monkey, and Ross brings up the fact that Joey was literally the poster boy for gonorrhea). **C**

19. The One With Joey's Award

PLOT Joey is nominated for a Soapie (the third-most-prestigious soap award). One of Ross's male students apparently has a crush on him. Monica freaks about all the stuff she'll have to give up for marriage. **BEST LINE** "You're getting married; this is all I have." (Rachel, vying with Monica to be Joey's Soapie date) **REVIEW** Oh, the delicious irony of watching the gang (who, aside from Kudrow up to this point, have been criminally deprived of deserved Emmys) riff on awards-show craziness, including the gracious-loser face. Kudos to Schwimmer for Ross's classroom impersonation of a raptor's high-pitched call. But overall a middling affair. **B**

20. The One With Ross and Monica's Cousin

PLOT Joey's auditioning for a movie that requires full-frontal nudity. M&C swear off sex until marriage. Ross and Monica's cousin Cassie visits. **CREATIVE CASTING** Denise Richards as Cassie. **BEST LINE** "A no-sex pact, huh? I actually have

one of those going on with every woman in America." (Ross) **REVIEW** The Cassie story is thin but effective: Chandler, Ross and even Phoebe get the hots for her, with Ross's seduction providing the most tickled ribs. Monica's attempts to fashion a foreskin for Joey (who needs one to get the part) pay off with a double-sided-tape-and-luncheon-meat joke and a perfect Silly Putty sight-gag kicker. **B+**

21. The One With Rachel's Big Kiss

PLOT Rachel kisses a girl. Chandler goes tux shopping at Ralph Lauren. **CREATIVE CASTING** Winona Ryder as Rachel's kissable sorority sis. **BEST LINE** "I was Chi Mega Tampon." (Phoebe, making up sorority roots) **REVIEW** There was some decent competition for best line honors (Monica's "A little tight? I could see double 0 and 7 in those," reaction to Chandler's Pierce Brosnan cast-off tux), but the tizzy over the women kissing is a little silly. **B-**

22. The One With the Vows

PLOT M&C's wedding-vow writer's block creates an excuse to flash back to the milestones of their relationship. **NEW DO** Chandler **BEST LINE** "Sweetie, you know I have no sense of humor when it comes to the wedding." (Monica) **REVIEW** A clip show that manages to amuse and tug at the heart-strings. After all, who can resist another shot of Chandler's Flock of Seagulls college hairdo and that candlelit proposal? **B+**

23. The One With Chandler's Dad

PLOT Monica arranges a trip to Vegas so Chandler can patch things up with his parent and invite her to the wedding. Rachel commandeers Monica's Porsche. **INTRODUCES** Kathleen Turner as Chandler's parent. **CREATIVE CASTING** Mark Consuelos (*All My Children*) as the cop who stops Rachel. Alexis Arquette (Courteney's former sis-in-law) as a snippy server at the drag show. **BEST LINE** "It's all very 'cat's in the cradle,' I don't want to get into it." (Chandler, on his relationship with his parent) **REVIEW** Despite a fun turn by Turner, the repeated confusion (or ignorance) over pronouns is cringe-inducing. And the Porsche plot stalls. **B-**

24-25. The One With Monica and Chandler's Wedding, Parts 1 & 2

PLOT Chandler, who picks the night before his wedding to start flipping out about marriage, goes MIA. Speaking of which: Joey gets a role in a WWI-themed movie. **CREATIVE CASTING** Gary Oldman as the actor playing opposite Joey. **BEST LINE** "Don't worry. We found the vest. I mean, we're going to have to keep an eye on it to make sure we don't lose it again." (Phoebe, covering for Chandler) **REVIEW** It may be M&C's big day, but Ross (who sweetly coaxes the butterflies out of Chandler) and Rachel (who appears to be holding the short end of a positive pregnancy-test stick—genius!) practically walk off with the show. Still, the couple of the hour do goose your tear ducts with their touching wedding vows. But what could have been an A episode is mired by Joey and Oldman's ludicrous on-set adventures and several insensitive jokes at Turner's character's expense. **B**

SEASON 8

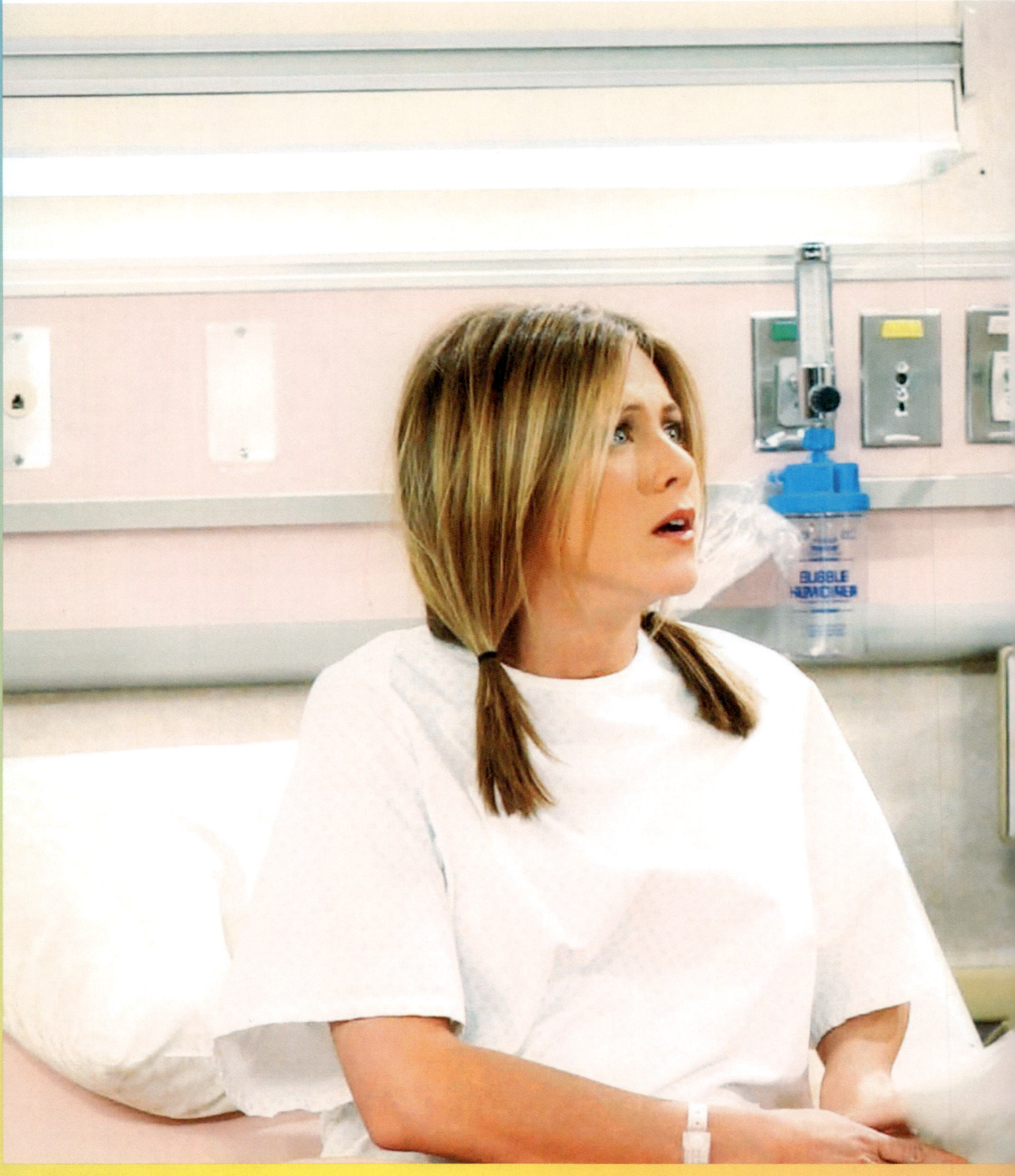

Great Expectations

Rachel is pregnant and wants to maintain a sense of 'normalcy' for as long as possible. But the development creates complications in a number of love lives

Rachel and Ross share a moment in the hospital before becoming parents.

RACHEL'S PREGNANCY BOTH INJECTED NEW LIFE INTO THE SERIES, and had ramifications offscreen too: Jennifer Aniston became just the second of the show's stars to win an Emmy. (Season 8 also marked the only time the show won for Outstanding Comedy Series.)

1. The One After 'I Do'

PLOT The discovery of Rachel's positive pregnancy test upends Monica and Chandler's wedding reception. To buy Rachel time to come to terms with her new future, Phoebe confesses she's the one who's expecting—with actor James Brolin. Ross's ploy to chat up Mona lands him at the kids' table, while Chandler struggles on the dance floor. **INTRODUCES** Bonnie Somerville as Mona **BEST LINE** "I have surprisingly small feet, but the rest of me is good—I'll show you!" (Joey, admitting to Chandler that he wears a size 7 shoe). **REVIEW** Aniston is superb as an emotional Rachel; Kudrow gets similarly high marks as her extra-supportive pal. **A-**

2. The One With the Red Sweater

PLOT After the disposable cameras from the reception go missing, Ross and Chandler crash a wedding to stage a makeup photo shoot, while Monica combats post-bridal gloom by feverishly opening gifts. Desperate to know who fathered Rachel's baby, Phoebe tries to track down the owner of a sweater Joey discovered in their apartment several weeks prior—which wrongly leads her to Tag. The mystery is solved when Ross claims the garment, saying "I've been looking for this for like a month!" **BEST LINE** "Marriage advice? Really?" (Chandler, to thrice-divorced Ross) **REVIEW** One of the best and most significant reveals in the show's history, pulled off with aplomb. **A-**

3. The One Where Rachel Tells...

PLOT When Rachel reveals her pregnancy to Ross, he goes into meltdown mode. Once things sink in, he shows up to her doctor's appointment, where they share a tender moment over the sonogram results. Monica and Chandler compete with another honeymooning couple for freebies, leaving Joey and Phoebe to find a way to break into their apartment and retrieve her guitar. **BEST LINE**... (Ross's expression as he sits in stunned silence after Rachel breaks the news) **REVIEW** Schwimmer steals the show, playing clueless, indignant, outraged and sweet; the Monica/Chandler story line falls flat. **B+**

4. The One With the Videotape

PLOT The gang press for details about their friends' one-night stand, but Rachel denies Ross's claim that she initiated their tryst—prompting Ross to admit that he accidentally videotaped their evening (he had been using Joey's camera to record himself practicing his seduction game, hoping to improve his technique). Ross is proven right when the tape shows Rachel using Joey's fictitious anecdote about backpacking through Western Europe, the story that never fails to lead to sex. **BEST LINE** "There he is now, the father of my child, the porn king of the West Village." (Rachel) **REVIEW** A laugh-out-loud installment that gets bonus points for a subplot in which Monica and Chandler's new couple friends try to ditch them. **A**

1

3

5. The One With Rachel's Date

PLOT Phoebe dates a sous chef at Monica's restaurant, only to feel smothered by him. But breaking off the relationship gets complicated when Monica decides to fire him—leaving them to quarrel over who can dump the guy first. Chandler stands in the way of a promotion for his coworker Bob (Chris Parnell), who has been

mistakenly calling Chandler "Toby" for years, and experiences unforeseen consequences. Rachel is delighted to score a date with one of Joey's *Days of Our Lives* costars—but Ross is horrified. His spirits lift when he runs into Mona at Central Perk. **BEST LINE** "Could be worse—it's not like he's calling me Muriel." (Chandler, inadvertently revealing his middle name) **REVIEW** Pleasantly diverting **B**

1. Rachel gets emotional over her positive pregnancy test with Phoebe and Monica. **3.** Ross joins Rachel for her doctor's visit. **6.** A costumed Monica and Chandler arm wrestle.

6. The One With the Halloween Party

PLOT Monica throws a last-minute costume party, where Ross, wearing a potato bodysuit and an antenna as "Spud-nik," and Chandler, dressed in a pink bunny outfit, arm wrestle to prove who is stronger. Smitten with Ursula's idealistic, if gullible, fiancé, Eric, Phoebe is upset to discover that Ursula's completely misrepresented herself to him. While handing out candy to trick-or-treaters, Rachel frets that maybe she's not so great with children. **CREATIVE CASTING** Sean Penn as Eric **BEST LINE** "Oh God! Chandler is making his sex face!" (Monica, watching her new hubbie try to pin Ross) **REVIEW** Kudrow, as always, nails her dual roles; she and Penn have terrific chemistry **A-**

7. The One With the Stain

PLOT To help Rachel land an apartment in his building, Ross pretends to have been close friends with a dying elderly woman—a ploy that forces him to learn some Dutch—but Joey wants her to stay at their place, even after the baby comes. Eric invites Phoebe to lunch, but her resemblance to Ursula causes serious problems. Monica becomes convinced the new maid Chandler hired is stealing her clothes. **BEST LINE** "'Relinquish' is just a fancy word for 'lose.'" (Monica, obviously) **REVIEW** An overly "sitcomy" vibe makes this one a lesser entry. **C+**

8. The One With the Stripper

PLOT Riddled with guilt that she refused to allow Chandler to have a bachelor party, Monica hires a stripper for him—but the woman turns out to be a sex worker. Rachel recruits Phoebe to join her for dinner with her overbearing father (Ron Leibman), who is furious to learn she's pregnant and that she and Ross aren't getting married. He storms over to Ross's apartment, interrupting his date with Mona. **BEST LINE** "Sure, one year is paper, but two months is lap dance." (Ross) **REVIEW** Aniston is superb playing opposite Leibman's hilarious hothead; Perry and LeBlanc shine as the befuddled BFFs. **B+**

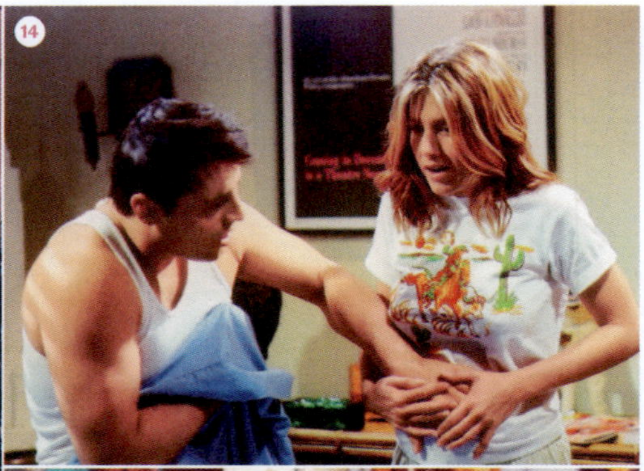

13. The gang walk in on Chandler in the bath. **14.** Joey feels the baby kick. **15.** Monica, Rachel and Chandler get an eyeful of a birthing video.

↓ BEST EPISODE

9. The One With the Rumor

PLOT Monica invites an old friend, Will (Brad Pitt), to Thanksgiving dinner—remarking to the gang that he, like her, has lost a significant amount of weight since high school. But things get off to a rocky start when Monica mentions that Rachel will be joining them for the meal. Tensions continue to rise until it comes out that Will and Ross were the co-founders of the "I Hate Rachel Green" club—not only that, but they also started a rumor that she had both male and female reproductive organs. Joey plans to consume an entire turkey, eventually trading his jeans for Phoebe's old maternity pants. **BEST LINES** "My two greatest enemies, Ross. Rachel Green and complex carbohydrates." (Will) "Come on, Will! Just take off your shirt and tell us." (Phoebe) **REVIEW** Yes, the rumor is problematic, but the cast is uniformly excellent in an episode that cleverly harnesses Pitt's star power for comedy gold—the Oscar winner netted an Emmy nom for his guest-star turn, which also marked the only time he and then-wife Aniston ever shared the screen. **A**

10. The One With Monica's Boots

PLOT To justify buying a pair of expensive boots, Monica vows to wear them all the time, but they're so painful she can barely walk in them. Joey hits the roof when he finds out his little sister Dina (Marla Sokoloff) is pregnant—a reaction entirely at odds with his supportive stance toward Rachel. When Phoebe discovers that Ross's son and Sting's son attend the same school, she urges Ross to hit up the musician for concert tickets. **BEST LINE** "The guy who made these hates feet and wants to see them die." (Monica) **REVIEW** Maybe limit the unplanned pregnancies to one per season? After Penn and Pitt, the parade of guest stars (Sting's wife, Trudie Styler, cameos) begins to feel gimmicky. **B-**

11. The One With Ross's Step Forward aka the One With the Creepy Christmas Card

PLOT Mona's idea to send out a joint holiday card with Ross leads to a verrryyyy uncomfortable conversation about the state of their relationship. To get Monica out of going to dinner with his boorish boss Doug (Sam McMurray), Chandler says they've split up—prompting Doug to take Chandler out to a strip club. Rachel's pregnancy hormones have her lusting after every guy she sees, possibly even Joey. **BEST LINE** "Lately with this whole pregnancy thing, I'm just finding myself, how do I put this? Erotically charged." (Rachel) **REVIEW** Aniston is great as randy Rachel, but it's little excruciating to see Schwimmer's Ross squirm his way through "the talk." And the Chandler subplot is a dud. **C-**

12. The One Where Joey Dates Rachel

PLOT After Rachel mentions how much she misses dating, Joey takes her out on the town—prompting him to see his longtime friend in a new light. Phoebe's belated wedding gift of a classic Ms. Pac-Man machine creates trouble: Chandler's endless playing leaves his fingers frozen into a claw, and Monica and Phoebe race to beat his high scores, lest Ben reads the dirty words he's left on the initials screen. Ross struggles to make it to class on time. **BEST LINE** "I never thought I would say this about a movie, but I really hope this dog dies." (Rachel, watching the horror film *Cujo*) **REVIEW** LeBlanc and Aniston are fantastic in the installment that plants the seeds for the Joey-loves-Rachel story line. **B-**

13. The One Where Chandler Takes a Bath

PLOT Monica gets Chandler hooked on bubble baths. After deciding not to learn the sex of the baby, Rachel and Ross can't agree on possible names; believing she knows what they're having, he calls the doctor and finds out it's a girl—information he blurts out to a surprised but delighted Rachel. Phoebe talks to Joey about his crush. **BEST LINE** "That's a really pretty name for an industrial solvent." (Ross, when Rachel suggests the name "Sandrine.") **REVIEW** Frothy fun but not especially memorable. **C+**

14. The One With the Secret Closet

PLOT Chandler discovers neat-freak Monica's deepest, darkest secret: She's shoved countless items into a closet, which is now overflowing and in disarray. Ross is distraught over missing milestone moments in Rachel's pregnancy, so Joey reluctantly suggests that Rachel move in with him. Phoebe is taken aback by Monica's orgasmic reaction to a massage. **BEST LINE** "I don't love you because you're organized. I love you in spite of that." (Chandler) **REVIEW** Joey's nightmare about Rachel delivering a baby with Ross's face is unforgettable but not in a good way. **B-**

15. The One With the Birthing Video

PLOT Valentine's Day goes awry when Mona dumps Ross after finding out Rachel has moved in with him (did he honestly not see that coming?). Chandler and Monica's romantic plans are ruined after they accidentally watch a graphic birthing video Phoebe brought over. Joey tells Ross about his feelings for Rachel. **BEST LINE** "Oh my God! No wonder my mother hates me!" (Monica, watching the tape) **REVIEW** LeBlanc does yeoman's work as confused, lovestruck Joey, giving the character welcome depth and complexity. **B**

16. The One Where Joey Tells Rachel

PLOT When Joey tells Ross that he's love in with Rachel, Ross spins out, prompting Joey to ponder leaving "the country" (to move to Vermont). But Ross later advises his friend to talk to

↓ James Michael Tyler at Cafe Central Perk in New York in 2014.

Remembering James Michael Tyler

THE ACTOR, WHO PLAYED ACERBIC BARISTA GUNTHER, DIED IN 2021. ***By Amy Wilkinson***

"It was the most memorable 10 years of my life," actor James Michael Tyler said of playing Gunther, the Central Perk mainstay (and Rachel Green superfan). "I could not have imagined just a better experience."

That sentiment, shared via a Zoom appearance during HBO Max's 2021 *Friends: The Reunion*, would be one of the last times fans would hear from Tyler. He died later that year from prostate cancer at age 59.

Tyler's first (albeit brief) appearance as the bleach-blond coffee hawker was in *Friends'* second episode ("The One With the Sonogram at the End"), and he didn't get speaking lines until season 2. Tyler later explained he landed the role because he was the only extra on-set who knew how to work an espresso machine.

Gunther would be one of the few recurring characters to appear in all 10 seasons, and Tyler—who also had roles on *Scrubs* and *Sabrina the Teenage Witch*—recalled his time with the cast fondly. "All these guys were fantastic, and it was just a joy to work with them," he said. "I felt very, very special."

Rachel, pointing out that Joey deserves to know if she also has feelings for him. Over a romantic dinner, he learns that she doesn't, but the two share a lengthy embrace. Phoebe meets Monica's soulmate, a handsome British foodie. **BEST LINE** "Women never like Joey. You know, I think he's a virgin." (Ross, to Monica) **REVIEW** Schwimmer plays Ross's sputtering, stammering reaction to the hilt; Aniston is sincerely charming as an entirely caught-off-guard Rachel. **B+**

17. The One With the Tea Leaves

PLOT To get past the awkward silence that's sprung up between them, Rachel asks for Joey's help with a work problem—forced to make up something on the spot, she tells him her boss wants to buy her baby. Naturally Joey goes to her office to confront him, creating a whole new set of problems. Ross uses a spare key to let himself into Mona's apartment to retrieve his "faded salmon" (pink) shirt and has to hide when she comes home with a date. Phoebe goes to dinner with a man she's been seeing all around town, who turns out to be just awful. Monica and Chandler organize their CDs. **BEST LINE** "I'm not great at the advice. Can I interest you in a sarcastic comment?" (Chandler) **REVIEW** Rachel's ridiculous lie helps move the show beyond the angsty unrequited love plotline and get back to laugh-out-loud comedy. **A**

18. The One in Massapequa

PLOT The gang attend the Geller's 35th-anniversary party on Long Island, where Monica gives a toast designed to make her mother and father cry. To placate their parents, Ross and Rachel pretend to be married, leading Rachel to invent details of an elaborate destination wedding with entertainment by Stevie Wonder. Phoebe's oppressively optimistic date Parker proves far too upbeat, even for her. **CREATIVE CASTING** Alec Baldwin as Parker **BEST LINE** "I'm a positive person. You are like Santa Claus on Prozac at Disneyland getting laid." (Phoebe) **REVIEW** Although Kudrow shines as the eternally sunny friend pushed past her breaking point, this one sorta feels like attending a party you'd like to leave early. **C**

19. The One With Joey's Interview

PLOT Joey is interviewed by a *Soap Opera Digest* reporter, and the gang sit close by to stop him from saying anything stupid—a plan that almost works. **BEST LINE** "In my spare time, I read to the blind, and I'm also a Mento for kids." (Joey, of course) **REVIEW** Essentially a clip show, with each question prompting Joey to reflect on various memories; too many flashbacks make this a glorified rerun. **C-**

20. The One With the Baby Shower

PLOT Monica and Phoebe throw Rachel a shower but forget to invite her mom until the last minute—leaving Monica to atone for the oversight. When Rachel panics that she won't be able to care for the baby, mom Sandra offers to move in to help. Ross and Chandler pretend to be contestants on a confusing game show called Bamboozled to get Joey ready for an audition. **BEST LINE** "You mean they're not coming to a social event where there's no men and no booze? That's shocking." (Rachel, learning her sisters won't make the shower) **REVIEW** Both story lines are a riot,

Marlo Thomas's judgmental Sandra is a scream, and there's even a sweetly sincere moment with Ross reassuring Rachel that she will be a great mom. **A**

21. The One With the Cooking Class

PLOT Rachel is consumed with jealousy when Ross goes for a coffee date with a salesclerk from the store where they were shopping for baby gear (who, upon learning that Ross is a paleontologist, compares him to Indiana Jones). To regain her confidence after a bad review, Monica, with Joey in tow, confronts the food critic at a local community college where he teaches, only to wind up as the star student in a beginner-level cooking class. Phoebe helps prep Chandler for a job interview. **BEST LINE** "You would date a gorilla

20

23

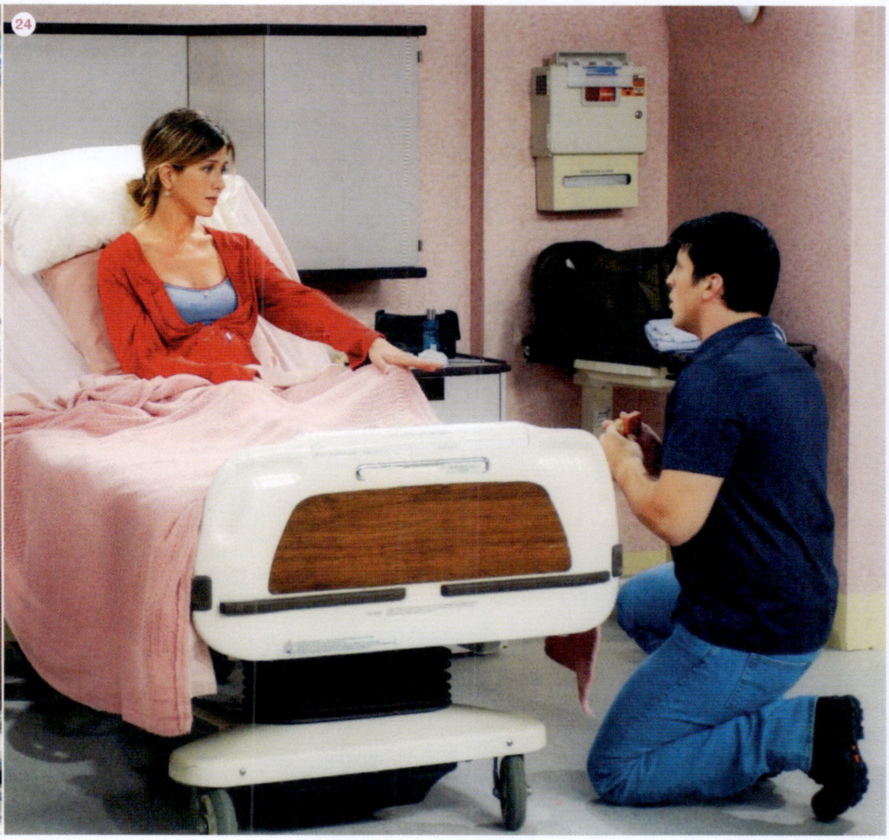
24

if it called you Indiana Jones." (Rachel) **REVIEW** Rachel's over-the-top spitefulness and Monica's over-the-top neediness are kind of a drag to watch in this just-okay installment. **B-**

22. The One Where Rachel Is Late

PLOT One week past her due date, a miserable Rachel is willing to try anything to trigger labor; when her doctor suggests sex, Rachel attempts to harangue Ross into sleeping with her. Chandler dozes off during the premiere of Joey's World War I movie; Phoebe and Monica bet on what day the baby will be born. **BEST LINE** "We should probably ask the doctor if she even knows how to deliver a baby that's half human half pure evil." (Ross) **REVIEW** Aniston and Schwimmer's back-and-forth takes center stage, but each friend makes the most of solid material that plays to their respective strengths. **A**

17. Alec Baldwin guest-stars as Phoebe's overly enthusiastic date. **20.** Sandra (Marlo Thomas) at Rachel's baby shower **23.** Monica and Chandler search for a place to get busy in the hospital. **24.** Joey unwittingly proposes to Rachel.

23. The One Where Rachel Has a Baby, Part 1

PLOT After going into labor at last, Rachel shares a semiprivate hospital room with a parade of oddball couples—including Janice (!) and her new husband. Monica and Chandler decide to try to have a baby of their own and frantically search for a room where they can have sex. Joey poses as Dr. Drake Ramoray to help Phoebe track down a cute guy she meets in the hallway. Ross's mom turns up with an heirloom engagement ring for Ross to present to Rachel. **BEST LINE** "Three hours and still no baby.... The miracle of birth sure is a snoozefest." (Phoebe) **REVIEW** Many series have done "the birth episode"—few have done it this well. **A**

24. The One Where Rachel Has a Baby, Part 2

PLOT Rachel delivers baby girl Emma (her name courtesy of Monica). Phoebe pushes Ross to reconsider being with Rachel, while Janice suggests that Rachel should be prepared to raise their baby on her own, as Ross will likely start a family with another woman one day. Joey accidentally proposes to Rachel with the ring that falls out of Ross's jacket pocket—and she accepts. **BEST LINE** "She's amazing. Oh, I'm so glad you guys got drunk and had sex." (Monica, holding her new niece) **REVIEW** So funny and moving that we'll forgive the ring mix-up at the end. **A** EW

SEASON 9

Family Matters

Ross and Rachel commit to co-parenting daughter Emma, and Chandler and Monica start trying to have a baby of their own

Monica seems to be the only one who can quiet a crying baby Emma.

FOR THE FINAL TWO SEASONS OF the show, the cast asked for $1 million each per episode. Knowing how valuable the Must See TV show was to their lineup—and bottom line—the network agreed.

1. The One Where No One Proposes

PLOT Poor Rachel: Just hours after giving birth, she's forced to deal with two man babies—Ross and Joey—who can't seem to resolve the mistaken proposal thing. Meanwhile, Jack gets an eyeful of his little Harmonica having sex in a hospital closet with Chandler in the hopes of conceiving. **BEST LINE** "Ross had a ring, and he was going to propose?... And you did it first? This is going to kill him. You know how much he loves to propose." (Chandler, to Joey) **REVIEW** Okay, the whole ring thing does start to wear thin (how many times can someone barge into Rachel's hospital room!?), but Elliott Gould provides some welcome carnal comic relief. **B**

2. The One Where Emma Cries

PLOT Ross and Rachel bring their baby home, but she won't stop wailing. To make up for proposing to Rachel, Joey tells Ross to hit him—but he ducks at the last moment, and Ross punches a metal pole instead, sending him to the hospital. After falling asleep during a staff meeting, Chandler unwittingly agrees to run the company's Tulsa office, but Monica doesn't want to move. **BEST LINE** "This just proves no good can come from having sex with Ross." (Phoebe, about Emma's crying) **REVIEW** The episode balances the extremes of slapstick comedy and new-parenthood anxiety well. And Joey not understanding air quotes is a riot. **A-**

3. The One With the Pediatrician

PLOT After placing incessant phone calls, Rachel gets dumped... by her baby's doctor. She asks Ross about his former pediatrician, but he lies and says he died to cover up the fact that he is still being treated by him. Phoebe and Joey agree to set each other up, but he forgets to find a date for Phoebe and picks up a stranger at Central Perk. Monica decides not to move to Tulsa after she's offered a primo new job in New York. **NEW DO** Monica **INTRODUCES** Paul Rudd as Phoebe's musician beau Mike. **BEST LINE** "There's no guys in there." (Joey, looking through his phone book for a date for Phoebe) **REVIEW** In just a few short scenes, Rudd manages to charm (hello, air piano) and gives Phoebe—finally—a worthy suitor. **A-**

4. The One With the Sharks

PLOT To keep their long-distance relationship spicy, Monica shows up to Chandler's Tulsa hotel room unannounced and finds him getting off—she thinks—to a shark-attack video. Ross accidentally spills the beans to Mike that Phoebe has never been in a serious relationship but tries to backpedal with a story about Phoebe's ex "Vikram." **BEST LINE**

1. Joey tries to explain himself to Rachel and Ross. **2.** Chandler dozes and ends up accepting a work assignment he does not want. **4.** Mike (Paul Rudd) and Phoebe hit it off.

"What' means, like, if he gets a disease or kills someone, not if he gets his jollies to *Jaws*." (Monica, on her vows to love Chandler no matter what) **REVIEW** Monica's well-meaning (albeit misguided) attempts to satisfy Chandler's shark cravings are hysterical, and good on Mike for sticking it out with Phoebe despite all of Ross's annoying bungles. **A-**

5. The One With Phoebe's Birthday Dinner

PLOT Phoebe and Joey try holding down a table for six while the rest of the gang are running late—Rachel and Ross have locked themselves out of the apartment with Emma inside; Monica and Chandler are fighting over his renewed smoking habit. **BEST LINE** "Dinner for six for one? You boys are about to see something special." (Joey, left with all of the gang's entrées) **REVIEW** It's hard not to compare "TOWPBD" to season 3's superior "The One Where No One's Ready," which did the one-friend-waiting-for-everyone-else conceit more deftly. **B**

6. The One With the Male Nanny

PLOT Ross's retro attitudes about gender norms rear their ugly head again when Rachel wants to hire a nanny who happens to be a man. Mike gives Phoebe the key to his apartment, and she reciprocates. But talk about timing: Just hours later Phoebe's ex David (Azaria) unexpectedly returns from Minsk. Chandler tries to out-funny Monica's new coworker. **CREATIVE CASTING** Freddie Prinze Jr. as nanny Sandy. **BEST LINE** "I can't watch—it's like firing Elmo." (Rachel) **REVIEW** Prinze Jr. is adorable as Sandy, but Ross's macho machinations bring the whole thing down. And the blah Phoebe and Chandler story lines don't help. **B-**

7. The One With Ross's Inappropriate Song

PLOT Ross sings a Sir Mix-a-Lot song to Emma, provoking her very first laugh. Rachel's peeved until she gets desperate for a chuckle and raps the same tune. Phoebe meets Mike's Upper East Side parents and keeps saying all the wrong things. **HISTORIC MOMENT** Phoebe and Mike share their first "I love you's." **BEST LINE** "When he gets going, he can rattle a headboard like a sailor on leave." (Phoebe, trying to make small talk with Mike's mom) **REVIEW** The "Baby Got Back" shenanigans are silly fun, and Lisa Kudrow cosplaying a member of the upper crust is winning. **B+**

8. The One With Rachel's Other Sister

PLOT It's Thanksgiving, and Rachel's self-obsessed sister Amy turns up at her door with nowhere to go. Rachel invites her over to Monica's, where they spend most of dinner arguing over who will get baby Emma if Ross and Rachel both die. Meanwhile, anxious Monica is worried someone is going to break a piece of her wedding china. **INTRODUCES** Christina Applegate as Rachel's sister. **BEST LINE** "Sure, Ross.

Yeah, if I have a heart attack at a restaurant, I want you there with your fossil brush." (Rachel to Ross after he says a Ph.D. is as good as an M.D.) **REVIEW** Applegate is great as a what-if version of Rachel had she never left Barry. But as far as Thanksgiving episodes go, this is certainly not the show's strongest serving. **B-**

9. The One With Rachel's Phone Number

PLOT Rachel and Phoebe go out for a girls' night, leaving Ross and Mike to have the most awkward boys' night on record. Instead of straightforwardly canceling plans with Joey, Chandler lies and says he has to stay in Tulsa, leading Joey to think Monica's having an affair with a guy he hears through her apartment door. **BEST LINE** "Eye contact? I hope you were using protection." (Phoebe, on Rachel and Ross's "moment") **REVIEW** Classic *Friends'* high jinks with a side of pathos, as Ross intercepts a call for Rachel from "Bill from the Bar" and doesn't give her the message. **B+**

10. The One With Christmas in Tulsa

PLOT Chandler is stuck in Oklahoma for the holidays (cue clips of Christmases of yore in New York!) and ultimately quits his job so he can fly home to be with Monica. **CREATIVE CASTING** Selma Blair as Chandler's Tulsa colleague Wendy. **BEST LINE** "Wait a minute. Am I sexy in Oklahoma?" (Chandler, after being hit on by Wendy) **REVIEW** It's not the shiniest present under the tree, but the episode at least wraps up that random Tulsa plot. **B**

11. The One Where Rachel Goes Back to Work

PLOT When Rachel returns to Ralph Lauren, she meets her

Are You Sure About That?

WITH 236 EPISODES, WRITERS ARE BOUND TO MAKE A CONTINUITY ERROR EVERY NOW AND THEN. HERE ARE A FEW NOTABLE FLUBS

1. FAMILY TIES
In "The One With Mrs. Bing," Joey says it's never okay to kiss moms, though aunts and sisters are possible. But later Tribbiani's reaction to Chandler's bussing his sis ("The One Where Chandler Can't Remember Which Sister") is not so familial.

2. WHO'S FIRST?
In "The One With Rachel's Assistant," Chandler reveals that Ross slept with a cleaning woman in college. But in "The One With Phoebe's Husband," Ross makes a big deal about how Carol was the only woman he'd slept with until Julie.

3. CAR TROUBLE
Ross's dad says he got his Porsche when he turned 50 ("The One Where Joey Moves Out"). But in "The One With All the Rugby," Ross mentions how, when he was 4, he "washed my dad's Porsche with rocks." But that would mean sixtysomething Elliott Gould is actually playing someone much older.

4. SPELL CHECK
When Ross sends Rachel a wedding invitation ("The One With the Invitation"), the envelope is addressed "Rachel Greene." You'd think he'd know the love of his life spells it "Green."

5. TO THE DOGS
Chandler has a thing against pooches, as we find out in "The One Where Chandler Doesn't Like Dogs." Interesting, then, that he was perfectly calm when Phoebe toted around her mom's puppy ("The One With Phoebe's Uterus").

6. EYE WARY
Rachel is freaked out by eyeballs, to the point where she can't even look when someone touches their own eye ("The One With Joey's Big Break"). But in "The One With Chandler in a Box," Rachel readily comes to Monica's aid when she gets an ice fragment lodged in her peeper—even taking Monica to the eye doctor's office and joking about jamming a pen into her eye.

7. CHANCY MEETINGS
Who knew whom, and when did they know them? As we learn in "The One With All the Thanksgivings," Chandler and Rachel met several times at the Gellers' house during Thanksgiving breaks while Chandler was in college and Rachel was in high school. So why is it that they have no idea who the other one is when they run into each other at the pre-Central Perk bar in "The One With the Flashback"? Guess it's not just the writers who have short memories.

cocky maternity-leave fill-in Gavin, who she thinks is trying to permanently replace her. A cash-strapped Phoebe takes on a job as an extra on *Days of Our Lives*, and Chandler is offered an unpaid internship for an advertising agency. **INTRODUCES** Dermot Mulroney as Gavin. **BEST LINE** "I learned to never borrow money from friends. No, that's why Richard Dreyfuss and I don't speak anymore." (Phoebe) **REVIEW** Phoebe-Joey story lines are always a crowd-pleaser, and Rachel and Gavin share a sexy adversarial energy. **A-**

10. Chandler's Tulsa colleague (played by Selma Blair) makes a pass at him. **11.** Rachel spars with coworker Gavin (Dermot Mulroney). **13.** Joey gets his eyebrow done. Yes, eyebrow. The pain was too much to let the aesthetician do the second one.

12. The One With Phoebe's Rats

PLOT Ross and Rachel hire a "hot" nanny (Melissa George), whom Ross tries to keep away from Joey. Phoebe's been leaving food out for a rodent visitor she's named Bob. Gavin makes a belated appearance at Rachel's birthday party—and kisses her. **BEST LINE** "Shhh! Don't say that loud. Gunther's going to want to hug me." (Rachel, being wished a happy birthday) **REVIEW** Joey chasing a pretty girl isn't exactly groundbreaking stuff, and Ross's continuing aggravation over Rachel potentially seeing other men is kind of unfair. **B**

13. The One Where Monica Sings

PLOT Reeling from seeing Rachel kissing Gavin, Ross decides he's moving on—unsurprisingly, he's awful at picking up women. Monica takes the mic at a piano bar, but it's her see-through top that gets the crowd cheering. Joey goes to get his eyebrows plucked for his new headshots. **BEST LINE** "You know when 'that's fine' sounds true? When someone yells it and spits!" (Chandler, to Ross) **REVIEW** Ross and Rachel finally talking about their complicated relationship is long overdue and sets the season in a new direction. **B+**

14. The One With the Blind Dates

PLOT In a bid to get Ross and Rachel back together, Joey and Phoebe set them up on horrible dates. Monica and Chandler agree to babysit Emma, but Monica's ovulating, so they briefly leave the baby unattended in the living room to have sex. Joey finds the solo Emma and takes her back to his place. **CREATIVE CASTING** Jon Lovitz returns as stoner Steve, who takes Rachel out. **BEST LINE** "We are very hip, happening people. Now, if you will excuse me, I have to get back to reading the obituaries." (Chandler) **REVIEW** The Lovitz callback is a fun bit of *Friends* fan service, and it's nice to see Ross and Rachel commiserating after the angst of the last episode. **B+**

↓ **BEST EPISODE**

15. The One With the Mugging

PLOT Chandler starts an unpaid advertising training program, and he's the oldest one in the group. Joey auditions for a Broadway play with famed actor/cell phone hawker Leonard Hayes, who has lots of notes for him. Phoebe and Ross get mugged, but she knows the perp from her street days. **CREATIVE CASTING** Jeff Goldblum as Leonard Hayes. **BEST LINE** "Oh,

c'mon, people, c'mon now. If I don't know who makes the most, I don't know who I like the most." (Phoebe) **REVIEW** Retconning a beloved piece of IP can have mixed results, but a teenage Phoebe having mugged a teenage Ross is genius. And Goldblum is especially Goldblummy in his guest turn. No weak story lines to be found in this one. **A**

16. The One With the Boob Job

PLOT Monica and Chandler separately (and secretly) ask to borrow money from Joey, as they're struggling financially. When Chandler finds out about Monica's ask, Joey lies and says it was for a boob job. Phoebe and Mike discuss moving in together. Rachel has the apartment baby-proofed, which effectively makes the apartment Joey-proof too. **BEST LINE** "I am warm for your form." (Chandler, trying to dissuade Monica from a boob job) **REVIEW** Chandler falling for the boob job lie seems unrealistic, but Phoebe and Ross's heart-to-heart—and her breakup with Mike—add emotional heft to the episode. **B+**

17. The One With the Memorial Service

PLOT Ross and Chandler hack each other's alumni profiles in an escalating prank war, concluding in Ross's "death" and memorial service. Phoebe is grieving over her breakup with Mike. Joey doesn't like Emma playing with his stuffed penguin Hugsy. **BEST LINE** "Wait a second. You split with Carol because you had different interests? I think you split with Carol because you had one very similar interest." (Chandler, to Ross) **REVIEW** The faux memorial service gag is ludicrous. **C**

15. Phoebe reunites with old friend Lowell (Kyle Gass, left) in an unorthodox way. **16.** The gang confront Joey about his boob job lie. **20.** Ross meets his new colleague Charlie (Aisha Tyler). **23.** Phoebe gets back together with David (Hank Azaria), who's back from Minsk. **24.** Joey and Rachel finally get together in Barbados.

18. The One With the Lottery

PLOT The gang (sans party pooper Ross) pool their funds to buy a pile of $300 million Powerball tickets. Chandler is waiting to hear if he got a full-time role at his ad agency. **BEST LINE** "Get ready to hear a lot of boohockey, gosh darn it and brother pucker." (Rachel, on sanitizing their language for

24

Emma) **REVIEW** Chandler hitting the career jackpot is the highlight of this episode. **B**

19. The One With Rachel's Dream

PLOT After watching Joey film a romantic scene on *Days of Our Lives*, Rachel has a spicy dream about her friend. Chandler takes Ross on the romantic Vermont trip he had planned for him and Monica. Back at home, Monica is dealing with a busking Phoebe in front of her swanky restaurant. **BEST LINE** "Some of these people must have seen me play before, because they were requesting a bunch of my songs. Yeah, 'You Suck' and 'Shut Up and Go Home.'" (Phoebe, singing outside Monica's restaurant) **REVIEW** LeBlanc and Aniston turn in winning performances, and Ross and Chandler's hoarding of hotel amenities to recoup their bill is a hoot. **A-**

20. The One With the Soap Opera Party

PLOT Joey tries to use the ruse of tickets to a one-woman show to get the rest of the gang out for the night so he can throw a secret rooftop party for his costars. Ross meets a beautiful new colleague. **INTRODUCES** Aisha Tyler as Professor Charlie Wheeler. **CREATIVE CASTING** Alex Borstein as the one-woman-play actress. **BEST LINE** "I don't mean to pry. It is just that this must be what regular people experience when they watch *Access Hollywood*." (Ross, pumping Charlie for information about her Nobel-winning scientist ex) **REVIEW** The Joey-Charlie kiss at the episode's conclusion adds an interesting wrinkle to the romantic plotlines as they build toward the season finale. **A-**

21. The One With the Fertility Test

PLOT Phoebe rips up Rachel's gift certificate to a big corporate spa because they're evil money-hungry operations, but—plot twist!—Phoebe is actually working at said spa and is assigned to Rachel when she gets a massage anyway. Joey seeks out advice from Ross on how to wine and dine Charlie. Monica and Chandler go to a fertility clinic and run into Janice. **BEST LINE** "Who says wine has to cost more than milk?" (Joey) **REVIEW** The rare tearjerker from *Friends*. Chandler and Monica's fertility struggles serve as a poignant conclusion to the episode. **A-**

22. The One With the Donor

PLOT Monica and Chandler have a consult with their fertility doctor, who says their best options are surrogacy, a sperm donor or adoption. Chandler brings home his coworker Zack as a potential donor and makes things weird. Rachel confesses her Joey crush to Phoebe, and Charlie overhears. Ross's bid for keynote speaker goes awry when his adviser falls asleep mid-presentation. **CREATIVE CASTING** John Stamos as Zack. **BEST LINE** "I want to find a baby that needs a home and raise it with you. And I want to mess it up in our own specific way." (Chandler, to Monica) **REVIEW** Stamos's inherent charms could have been leveraged to greater effect, but Chandler and Monica's awkward interrogation of him is nonetheless a funny bit of business. **A-**

23–24. The One in Barbados, Parts 1 & 2

PLOT The gang head to the Caribbean for Ross's paleontology conference. Phoebe brings along David, with whom she's back together. Chandler's awful advice inspires David to propose to Phoebe, but Mike ultimately interrupts his plan, thanks to Monica's meddling. After Chandler accidentally erases Ross's speech by opening a spam email on his computer, Ross and Charlie hole up in his room to re-create it, and they have a blast. Feeling something for Ross, Charlie breaks up with Joey, who in turn kisses Rachel. Monica's hair gets big in the Barbados humidity. **BEST LINE** "Nude pictures of Anna Kournikova? I mean, she's never even won a major tournament." (Ross, to Chandler on the spam he clicked on) **REVIEW** So much happening in this two-parter. While the relationship whiplash is real, fans of the Rachel-Joey dynamic finally get their happy ending. At least for now. **A-** EW

SEASON 10

Saying Goodbye

It's the end of an era: Phoebe gets married, Monica and Chandler become parents, and Rachel and Ross get together—for good. (Oh, and Joey gets a spinoff)

A *Friends* tradition: Thanksgiving dinner with Ross, Phoebe, Joey, Monica, Chandler and Rachel.

IN AN ABBREVIATED 10TH SEASON, THE WRITERS WRAPPED UP THE show's lingering plotlines and delivered a memorable final installment that earned 52.5 million viewers, making it the fifth-most-watched series finale of all time.

1. The One After Joey and Rachel Kiss

PLOT Thanks to paper-thin walls, Monica, Chandler and Phoebe can hear new couples Joey and Rachel and Ross and Charlie making out in their adjacent hotel rooms. But before things can go any further, Ross decides he needs to talk to Joey (and vice versa). When the two finally chat on the plane ride home, Ross says his part, but Joey loses his nerve. In other relationship news, Mike has a girlfriend (and it's not Phoebe). **NEW DO** Monica gets cornrows (problematic, yes) **BEST LINE** "Ross and Charlie? Wow, she's really making her way through the group, huh? Well, who am I to talk?" (Rachel) **REVIEW** The goofy eavesdropping opener feels reminiscent of early *Friends* (in a good way), and the rest of the episode is pretty solid overall. **A-**

2. The One Where Ross Is Fine

PLOT After Ross walks in on Joey and Rachel kissing, he can't stop saying "I'm fine!" in an increasingly high-pitched tenor. He's so fine, in fact, that he proposes a double date with him and Charlie. Chandler and Monica meet with Phoebe's couple friends to get advice on adoption, and Chandler lets it slip to the couple's in-the-dark son that he's adopted. **BEST LINE** "I think everyone would feel better if we had some flan!" (Ross, drunk at his dinner party) **REVIEW** The Frank Jr. drop-in is random at best (did Giovanni Ribisi's film schedule open up or something?), but it's nice to see Joey continuing to mature and having an honest conversation with Ross. **B**

3. The One With Ross's Tan

PLOT Ross tries out spray-tanning but can't figure out the timing in the booth and gets hit four times on his front and zero times on his back. Rachel and Joey go out on their first official date, and when they start necking on the couch, Rachel keeps reflexively slapping

1. Chandler, Monica and Phoebe eavesdropping in Barbados. 2. Ross serves up a very awkward fajita night. 3. Monica and Phoebe try to cut out annoying friend Amanda (Jennifer Coolidge). 7. Ross persuades Rachel to give the swings a try.

Joey's hand off her thigh. Phoebe and Monica try cutting out their annoying, faux-British-accented friend Amanda, but she reveals that Phoebe once tried cutting Monica out. **CREATIVE CASTING** Jennifer Coolidge as Amanda **NEW DO** Monica **BEST LINE** "Stop staring at my wife's legs. No, no. Stop staring at your sister's legs." (Chandler, to Ross, who's admiring Monica's tan) **REVIEW** Leather pants, teeth-whitening, spray tanning—Ross's misadventures in style and grooming are always entertaining. Meanwhile, Joey's conclusion that he and Rachel are too good of friends to go there, is a real heart-warmer. **A-**

4. The One With the Cake

PLOT Monica and Chandler postpone their departure to Vermont so they can attend Emma's 1st-birthday party, but the fete is delayed while the 1-year-old naps. Further complicating matters: Ross discovers the birthday cake was accidentally baked in the shape of a penis rather than a bunny. **BEST LINE** "Remember, Emma, heart disease kills women too." (Judy Geller recording an 18th-birthday message for her granddaughter) **REVIEW** Much like Emma, this one is a bit of a snoozer. **B-**

5. The One Where Rachel's Sister Babysits

PLOT Amy turns up at Rachel's again, this time needing a place to live after breaking up with her rich older boyfriend. Joey volunteers to write a letter of recommendation for Monica and Chandler's adoption application, but he goes a little nuts with the thesaurus. When Emma's nanny cancels last-minute, Amy agrees to watch her niece—and pierces her ears. **HISTORIC MOMENT** Mike and Phoebe get engaged. **BEST LINE** "You'll love the feeling—there's nothing like it." (Ross, encouraging Phoebe to propose to Mike) **REVIEW** Christina Applegate turns in another memorable performance as ditzy Amy, and Phoebe finally finding her own lobster is long overdue. **A-**

6. The One With Ross's Grant

PLOT Ross is up for a $25,000 grant, but the head of the selection committee is Charlie's ex Dr. Benjamin Hobart, who pressures Ross to break up with Charlie. Chandler's working on his first national ad campaign, and Joey wants a role. Phoebe is clearing out space in her apartment for Mike to move in and must part with the creepy wall-hanging she's dubbed Gladys. Monica accidentally talks her way into taking it. **CREATIVE CASTING** Greg Kinnear (a *Talk Soup* host before Aisha Tyler) as Hobart. **BEST LINE** "I can't believe I'm about to meet Benjamin Hobart. I've always thought of him as one of the people I'd invite to my fantasy dinner party. Do you think there's any chance he'll bring Christie Brinkley or C-3PO?" (Ross) **REVIEW** The Gladys gag is the best part of this otherwise only okay episode. **B**

7. The One With the Home Study

PLOT An adoption worker comes over to assess Monica and Chandler as adoptive parents, but she's one of Joey's one-night stands whom he never called back. Phoebe decides to donate the money for her big wedding to a children's charity and have a small affair at city hall instead. But she changes her mind and has to go back to the charity for her check. Rachel is afraid of swings. **BEST LINE** "Hello, is this the Creepy residence?" (Phoebe, when Monica and Chandler open the door smiling for the adoption worker) **REVIEW** Once again, Joey's juvenile antics somehow manage to help Chandler and Monica in their adoption quest. Isn't it ironic? **B+**

8. The One With the Late Thanksgiving

PLOT Dinner's at 4, but Joey and Ross have Rangers tickets, and Phoebe persuades Rachel to enter Emma in a baby beauty pageant. When they all arrive late, a peeved Monica locks them out. **BEST LINE** "When I was here for Holidays on Ice, I was sitting so far away, Michelle Kwan couldn't read my banner." (Ross at Madison Square Garden) **REVIEW** The best Thanksgiving installments find the Friends all together in one room (or football field), so having them separated for the bulk of the half hour isn't very celebratory. But a well-timed call from the adoption agency (would they really be in the office on Thanksgiving?) ends the episode on a high note. **B+**

9. The One With the Birth Mother

PLOT Chandler and Monica fly to Ohio to meet a prospective birth mother, but there's some sort of mix up with the file—she thinks they're a doctor and a minister. Phoebe sets Joey up with a woman (Annie Parisse) who—gasp!—takes fries off his plate. **CREATIVE CASTING** Anna Faris as Erica, *Parks and Recreation* actor Jim O'Heir as the adoption agency employee **HISTORIC MOMENT** Erica picks Chandler and Monica **BEST LINE** "Joey doesn't share food!" (Joey) **REVIEW** The adoption agency screwup is a downer, but Chandler's moving plea at the end—and the couple's eventual triumph—gets you right in the tear ducts. **A-**

10. The One Where Chandler Gets Caught

PLOT Phoebe and Rachel think Chandler's having an affair when they spy him getting into a car with a blonde. But the woman is really his and Monica's real estate agent, who's found a home for them in Westchester. The gang are crestfallen to hear the couple will be leaving the city and relive their favorite moments in the apartment. **BEST LINE** "I want girls on bread!" (Joey when asked whether he'd give up food or sex—and can't decide) **REVIEW** You could fast-forward through the middle of this episode and not miss much. **B-**

11. The One Where the Stripper Cries

PLOT At an alumni event, Chandler gives Ross permission to break "the pact" and ask out their

The Postshow Role Call

FRIENDS SPRINGBOARDED ITS STARS TO FAME, FORTUNE AND EVEN MORE TV AND MOVIE ROLES. ***By Amy Wilkinson***

Jennifer Aniston
Aniston has enjoyed the most high-profile career post-*Friends*, landing roles in films such as *The Breakup*, *Horrible Bosses* and *Murder Mystery*. And she can currently be seen in Apple TV+'s *The Morning Show*, playing perky presenter Alex Levy (above).

Courteney Cox
In 2009 Cox won the role of single mom Jules Cobb on the cult-loved sitcom *Cougar Town*, which ran for six seasons. The actress also continues to reprise her role as journalist Gale Weathers in the *Scream* film franchise (above).

Lisa Kudrow
It's a testament to Kudrow's acting chops that she's originated not one but two iconic TV characters. After Phoebe, Kudrow landed the lead role on HBO's *The Comeback* as Valerie Cherish, who (meta alert!) is a former '90s sitcom actress.

Matt LeBlanc
LeBlanc's tenure as Joey Tribbiani continued for another two seasons with the spinoff *Joey*. Much like Kudrow, he would go on to send up his acting career playing "Matt LeBlanc" on Showtime's *Episodes* (above), co-created by *Friends* boss David Crane.

Matthew Perry
Perry has appeared in a number of TV projects over the years, including the short-lived *Studio 60 on the Sunset Strip* (above), *Go On* and *The Odd Couple*. He also played the adult version of Zac Efron in the 2009 movie *17 Again*.

David Schwimmer
Schwimmer was largely absent from the small screen in the decade following *Friends*, but he returned in the 2010s with a handful of roles, most notably playing O.J. Simpson attorney Robert Kardashian in 2016's *American Crime Story*.

9. Monica and Chandler meet prospective birth mother Erica (Anna Faris). 11. Danny DeVito guest-stars as a stripper 12. Phoebe says "I do" to Mike (Paul Rudd).

college crush Missy Goldberg. But as it turns out, Chandler didn't exactly keep his end of the deal back in the day. Joey is tapped to appear on *The $10,000 Pyramid*, and we probably don't need to tell you how poorly that goes. Rachel and Monica throw Phoebe a tasteful tea bachelorette, but she wants something a bit more raucous, so they order a stripper, who ends up being a little long in the tooth. **CREATIVE CASTING** Ellen Pompeo as Missy, Danny DeVito as the stripper **BEST LINE** "Did someone call for the long arm of the law? I should warn you, I have a concealed weapon! I hope you're familiar with this state's penal code!" (Officer Goodbody) **REVIEW** DeVito as Officer Goodbody is a riot, and it's nice of the writers to throw us one more flashback episode before the end. **A-**

12. The One With Phoebe's Wedding

PLOT BEST LINE It's Phoebe's big day, and (nearly) everyone has a role to play: Monica is wedding planning (of course), Joey is walking Pheebs down the aisle, and Rachel is a bridesmaid. That leaves Ross and Chandler to do…nothing. But then one of Mike's groomsmen cancels, and Rachel is given the responsibility of picking the fill-in. Monica's high-strung ways end up getting her fired as wedding planner, forcing Phoebe to manage all the last-minute details herself. In the end, none of it really matters as a blizzard shuts down the city. **HISTORIC MOMENT** Phoebe ties the knot, despite the weather. **BEST LINE** "I must have been in missile training the day they taught that." (Phoebe, on not knowing military time) **REVIEW** Weddings always make us emotional, and Phoebe deserves nothing but the best. **A-**

13. The One Where Joey Speaks French

PLOT Serial résumé fudger Joey is caught in another lie when he lands an audition for a French-speaking role. He enlists Phoebe to teach him the language of love. Rachel's dad has a heart attack, and she and Ross drive out to Long Island to be with him. Later, at Rachel's childhood home, she makes a pass at Ross who demurs, saying he doesn't want to take advantage of her. Erica comes to New York for a visit, during which Chandler and Monica learn their baby's biological father could be a college student…or a shovel murderer. **BEST LINE** "[*Giggles*] You're so sexy!" (Rachel, to a French-speaking Phoebe) **REVIEW** Joey totally and completely flubbing French is pretty funny, and the simmering Ross-Rachel heat is palpable. **A-**

14. The One With Princess Consuela

PLOT Career opportunities ahoy: Ross is up for tenure, and Rachel is interviewing at Gucci. The former gets the promotion, while the latter gets fired from Ralph Lauren. On her way out the door, Rachel runs into old coworker Mark, who says there might be an opening at Louis Vuitton. Monica and Chandler take Joey to see their new house in Westchester, where he points out imaginary flaws to deter them from moving in. While there, he meets the

house's 8-year-old inhabitant Mackenzie, who gives him some sage advice. **BEST LINE** "You said it was in escrow. I couldn't even find it on that map!" (Joey, on Chandler and Monica's new house) **CREATIVE CASTING** *Star Trek: The Next Generation*'s Brent Spiner as Rachel's Gucci interviewer; Craig Robinson as the name-change clerk; Dakota Fanning as Mackenzie **HISTORIC MOMENT** Phoebe changes her name to Princess Consuela Banana Hammock **REVIEW** Ross still holding a grudge against Mark is a bit absurd, but Joey's enlightenment via an 8-year-old and Phoebe's name change are winning gambits. **A**

15. The One Where Estelle Dies

PLOT The episode picks back up right where the last left off: Rachel announcing she's been offered a job with Louis Vuitton in Paris. In an ill-advised scheme to keep Rachel in New York, Ross pays a visit to her old Ralph Lauren boss to see if he can get her job back. Joey's agent dies, and to save him from the stress of it all, Phoebe poses as Estelle on the phone. Chandler and Monica take a look at the house for sale next to theirs and find Janice touring the property. **CREATIVE CASTING** Jane Lynch as a real estate agent **BEST LINE** "Unless Snoopy says it to Charlie Brown, I think we're okay." (Chandler, to Monica, who's worried Joey might read the news of his agent's death in the paper) **REVIEW** Rachel's growing astonishment over Ralph Lauren's job overtures is fun, and Joey's from-beyond-the-grave chats with Estelle are also good for a laugh. **A-**

16. The One With Rachel's Going Away Party

PLOT It's Rachel's last night in New York, and she uses the evening to pull each Friend aside to say her goodbyes. That is, everyone but Ross, who interprets her lack of recognition as a slight and storms out. Rachel follows and explains that she actually cares too much and doesn't know how to say goodbye to him. They kiss. Meanwhile, Erica goes into labor. **BEST LINE** "Ross, she's giving us her baby. She can eat *you* if she wants." (Monica, on Erica eating anything she wants in the hotel's minibar) **REVIEW** Let the waterworks begin! Aniston does fine work in this episode, and it's a smart narrative device letting each Friend have their moment. **A**

15. Chandler and Monica worry that Janice (Maggie Wheeler) might be their new neighbor. **16.** The guys start packing... sort of. **17.** The gang take one last look at Monica's empty apartment.

↓ **BEST EPISODE**

17. The Last One

PLOT After their night together, Ross wants to get back together, but Rachel thinks their romp was the perfect way to say goodbye. And Ross isn't the only one in a confessional mood: At Central Perk, Gunther tells Rachel he loves her. Joey buys a chick and a duck as a housewarming gift for Monica and Chandler, but they get stuck inside the foosball table. Phoebe drives Ross to the airport so he can stop Rachel from flying to Paris, but they mistakenly go to JFK instead of Newark. Phoebe tries intercepting Rachel by cell

phone and starts a panic on the plane about the left "philange," causing everyone to deplane. The delay allows Ross time to tell Rachel how he feels, and he begs her to not get onto the plane. But she does anyway. **HISTORIC MOMENT** Rachel gets off the plane! Chandler and Monica become parents…to twins! Joey welcomes Chick Jr. and Duck Jr.! **BEST LINE** "This guy at work gave me *Sex for Dummies* as a joke. Who's laughing now?!" (Ross, to Rachel on his new moves) **REVIEW** Could it really have been any other way? No, in the end, it was always going to be Ross and Rachel. Ten seasons of will-they-won't-they conclude with the couple back in each other's arms, saying goodbye to Monica and Chandler, who are packing up their belongings (and new babies) to relocate to the suburbs. One by one, they each leave their key on the counter of the empty Apartment 20 before heading out for one last coffee. Series finales don't get more bighearted than this. **A+** EW

ENTERTAINMENT WEEKLY
PRESIDENT Leah Wyar
GENERAL MANAGER Patrick Gomez
DESIGN DIRECTOR Chuck Kerr
DIRECTOR OF EDITORIAL OPERATIONS Alexandra Brez

FRIENDS
EDITORIAL DIRECTOR Kostya Kennedy
EDITION EDITOR Amy Wilkinson
ART DIRECTOR Aaron Morales
CONTRIBUTING ART DIRECTOR Greg Monfries
PHOTO EDITORS Steph Durante
WRITERS Kristen Baldwin, Rob Brunner, Jamie Bufalino, Clarissa Cruz, Mike Flaherty, Nicholas Fonseca, Bruce Fretts, Cynthia Grisolia, Samantha Highfill, Albert Kim, Allyssa Lee, Jolie Madan, Gina McIntyre, Maggie Murphy, Jessica Shaw, Missy Schwartz, Marc Snetiker, Josh Wolk, Fan Wong
REPORTER Daniel S. Levy
COPY DESK Joanann Scali (Chief), James Bradley (Deputy), Gabrielle Danchick, Richard Donnelly, Shakthi Jothianandan, Matt Weingarden
RESEARCH DIRECTOR Céline Wojtala
PREMEDIA TRAFFICKING SUPERVISOR Taylor Thomas
PREMEDIA IMAGING SPECIALIST Paige E. King
COLOR QUALITY ANALYST Sarah Schroeder

DOTDASH MEREDITH PREMIUM PUBLISHING
VICE PRESIDENT & GENERAL MANAGER Jeremy Biloon
VICE PRESIDENT, GROUP EDITORIAL DIRECTOR Stephen Orr
DIRECTOR, BRAND MARKETING Jean Kennedy
ASSOCIATE DIRECTOR, BRAND MARKETING Bryan Christian
SENIOR BRAND MANAGER Katherine Barnet

EDITORIAL DIRECTOR Kostya Kennedy
CREATIVE DIRECTOR Gary Stewart
DIRECTOR OF PHOTOGRAPHY Christina Lieberman
EDITORIAL OPERATIONS DIRECTOR Jamie Roth Major
MANAGER, EDITORIAL OPERATIONS Gina Scauzillo
SPECIAL THANKS Gabby Amello, Brad Beatson

Dotdash meredith · MPA THE ASSOCIATION OF MAGAZINE MEDIA

CREDITS: Front cover Photo12/7e Art/Warner Bros Television/Alamy **Back cover** (from top) Photo12/7e Art/Warner Bros Television/Alamy; Paul Drinkwater/NBCU Photo Bank/Getty Images (2) **1** NBCU Photo Bank/Getty Images **2-3** © Warner Bros./Collection Christophel/Alamy **4-5** (clockwise from left) Jeffrey Mayer/WireImage/Getty Images; Kevin Foy/Alamy; Jin Lee/Bloomberg/Getty Images; Flatiron Books; HBO Max/Warner Bros. Television/Album/Alamy **6-8** Reisig & Taylor/NBCU Photo Bank/Getty Images (2) **9** (from left) Reisig & Taylor/NBCU Photo Bank/Getty Images; NBCU Photo Bank/Getty Images (2) **10-11** (clockwise from top left) © Warner Bros./Courtesy Everett Collection; Reisig & Taylor/NBCU Photo Bank/Getty Images (2); Paul Drinkwater/NBCU Photo Bank/Getty Images **12-13** (from left) Reisig & Taylor/NBCU Photo Bank/Getty Images (2); © NBC (2) **14-15** NBCU Photo Bank/Getty Images **16-17** (clockwise from left) Alice S. Hall/NBCU Photo Bank/Getty Images; Gary Null/NBCU Photo Bank/Getty Images; © Warner Bros./Courtesy Everett Collection **18** © Warner Bros./Collection Christophel/Alamy **19** (clockwise from top left) © NBC, Courtesy Photofest; NBCU Photo Bank/Getty Images; Joseph Del Valle/NBCU Photo Bank/Getty Images **20-21** (clockwise from left) Paul Drinkwater/NBCU Photo Bank/Getty Images (2); Alice S. Hall/NBCU Photo Bank/Getty Images; Randy Tepper/NBCU Photo Bank/Getty Images **22-23** Paul Drinkwater/NBCU Photo Bank/Getty Images **24** (clockwise from top) © Warner Bros., Courtesy Photofest; Mike Ansell/NBCU Photo Bank/Getty Images; Gary Null/NBCU Photo Bank/Getty Images **25** Robert Isenberg/NBCU Photo Bank/Getty Images **26** NBCU Photo Bank/Getty Images **27** (clockwise from top left) Brian D. McLaughlin/NBCU Photo Bank/Getty Images; Paul Drinkwater/NBCU Photo Bank/Getty Images; © Warner Bros./Collection Christophel/Alamy **28-29** (clockwise from bottom left) © NBC (2); © Warner Bros./Courtesy Everett Collection **29** (from top) © NBC; Gary Null/NBCU Photo Bank/Getty Images **30-31** Gary Null/NBCU Photo Bank/Getty Images **32-33** (clockwise from left) NBCU Photo Bank/Getty Images; © NBC/Courtesy Everett Collection; Gary Null/NBCU Photo Bank/Getty Images (2) **34** (clockwise from left) J. Delvalle/NBCU Photo Bank/Getty Images; Chris Haston/NBCU Photo Bank/Getty Images; © Warner Bros./Courtesy Everett Collection **35** NBCU Photo Bank/Getty Images **36** (from top) Gary Null/NBCU Photo Bank/Getty Images; © Warner Bros./Courtesy Everett Collection **37** (from left) Paul Drinkwater/NBCU Photo Bank/Getty Images; © NBC (2) **38-39** NBCU Photo Bank/Getty Images **40-41** (clockwise from left) Gary Null/NBCU Photo Bank/Getty Images; NBCU Photo Bank/Getty Images; © Warner Bros., Courtesy Photofest; Paul Drinkwater/NBCU Photo Bank/Getty Images **42** Kevin Mazur/WireImage/Getty Images **43** (from left) © NBC (2); Alice S. Hall/NBCU Photo Bank/Getty Images **44-45** (clockwise from left) Gary Null/NBCU Photo Bank/Getty Images; © Warner Bros./Courtesy Everett Collection; © NBC **46-47** J. Delvalle/NBCU Photo Bank/Getty Images **48** (from top) J. Delvalle/NBCU Photo Bank/Getty Images; © NBC **49** Paul Drinkwater/NBCU Photo Bank/Getty Images **50** © Warner Bros./Collection Christophel/Alamy **51** (from left) © NBC (2); NBCU Photo Bank/Getty Images **52** (clockwise from top left) © NBC/Courtesy Everett Collection; Paul Drinkwater/NBCU Photo Bank/Getty Images; NBCU Photo Bank/Getty Images **53** (from top) NBCU Photo Bank/Getty Images; © NBC **54** (from top) Paul Drinkwater/NBCU Photo Bank/Getty Images; © NBC, Courtesy Photofest; © Warner Bros./Courtesy Everett Collection **55** (clockwise from top left) Danny Feld/NBCU Photo Bank/Getty Images; NBCU Photo Bank/Getty Images; Danny Feld/NBCU Photo Bank/Getty Images; NBCU Photo Bank/Getty Images (2) **56-57** © Warner Bros./Collection Christophel/Alamy **58-59** (clockwise from left) NBCU Photo Bank/Getty Images; Paul Drinkwater/NBCU Photo Bank/Getty Images; NBCU Photo Bank/Getty Images (2) **60** (clockwise from left) NBCU Photo Bank/Getty Images; Chris Haston/NBCU Photo Bank/Getty Images; © NBC **61** NBCU Photo Bank/Getty Images **62-63** (clockwise from left) © Warner Bros./Courtesy Everett Collection (2); Paul Drinkwater/NBCU Photo Bank/Getty Images; Paul Drinkwater/NBCU Photo Bank/Getty Images **64-65** Danny Feld/NBCU Photo Bank/Getty Images **66** NBCU Photo Bank/Getty Images **67** (clockwise from bottom left) © Warner Bros./Courtesy Everett Collection (2); NBCU Photo Bank/Getty Images **68** (clockwise from bottom left) NBCU Photo Bank/Getty Images; © NBC (5) **69** NBCU Photo Bank/Getty Images (3) **70** (clockwise from top left) © Warner Bros./Collection Christophel/Alamy; © Warner Bros./Courtesy Everett Collection (2) **71-73** Danny Feld/NBCU Photo Bank/Getty Images (2) **74-75** (clockwise from top) Danny Feld/NBCU Photo Bank/Getty Images; © Warner Bros./Courtesy Everett Collection; NBCU Photo Bank/Getty Images **76** (clockwise from left) NBCU Photo Bank/Getty Images (2); Danny Feld/NBCU Photo Bank/Getty Images **77** Simon Broll/dpa picture alliance/Alamy **78** NBCU Photo Bank/Getty Images **79** (clockwise from bottom left) Danny Feld/NBCU Photo Bank/Getty Images (2); NBCU Photo Bank/Getty Images **80-81** Danny Feld/NBCU Photo Bank/Getty Images **82-83** (from left) NBCU Photo Bank/Getty Images; Danny Feld/NBCU Photo Bank/Getty Images (2) **84** (clockwise from top left) © NBC; Paul Drinkwater/NBCU Photo Bank/Getty Images; NBCU Photo Bank/Getty Images (2) **85** (clockwise from top left) © NBC; NBCU Photo Bank/Getty Images; © Warner Bros./Courtesy Everett Collection **86** NBCU Photo Bank/Getty Images (4) **87** © Warner Bros./Courtesy Everett Collection **88-89** © Warner Bros., Courtesy Photofest **90-91** (clockwise from left) NBCU Photo Bank/Getty Images; © Warner Bros., Courtesy Photofest (2); © NBC, Courtesy Photofest **92** (clockwise from top left) © Apple TV+/Courtesy Everett Collection; © Paramount Pictures, Courtesy Photofest; © Sophie Mutevelian/Showtime/Courtesy Everett Collection; © Prashant Gupta/FX/Courtesy Everett Collection; © Chris Haston/Warner Bros. Television/Courtesy Everett Collection; © Colleen Hayes/HBO/Courtesy Everett Collection **93** (from left) NBCU Photo Bank/Getty Images (2); © Warner Bros./Collection Christophel/Alamy **94-95** (clockwise from top left) © Warner Bros., Courtesy Photofest; © Warner Bros./Collection Christophel/Alamy (2) **96** (from top) © HBO Max, Courtesy Photofest; © Terence Patrick/HBO Max/Courtesy Everett Collection

Jennifer Aniston, Courteney Cox, Matthew Perry, Lisa Kudrow, David Schwimmer, Matt LeBlanc and the Central Perk couch.

FRIENDS TO THE END

Reunited, and It Feels So Good

HBO Max's *Friends: The Reunion* got the gang back together for one more remarkable night of reminiscing. The laughter and the love endured. *By Amy Wilkinson*

SEVENTEEN YEARS AFTER WALKING out the front door of Apartment 20 for the last time, the Friends returned to the Warner Bros. lot in 2021 for an emotional reunion to recount the decade they spent filming the beloved NBC series. One by one—some with tears in their eyes—the stars arrived to the re-created set, embracing one another and marveling at the place they called home for so many years. (The only thing missing? Monica's original cookie jar, which Kudrow took with her after filming concluded.)

The cast felt the significance of the moment. "After the initial shock of being in the same room together, I think we just fell right into our same old joking around," David Schwimmer told host James Corden. "We're family."

The nearly two-hour special proved to be a true love letter to the series: part clip show, part behind-the-scenes tour and part sit-down interview, *Friends: The Reunion* gave fans the chance to relive so many favorite funny—and heartfelt—moments from all 10 seasons. And one thing proved crystal clear: These six were destined to be friends forever. "We have such a bond from this show and forged this very tight relationship," Lisa Kudrow said. "Any time you text or call anyone, they'll be there." EW

↓ **From left** LeBlanc greeted Cox with a big hug; Schwimmer revived his role of quiz-show host in a callback to the season 4 episode "The One With the Embryos."

Printed in Dunstable, United Kingdom

82710554R00056